DISCOVER CANADA

British Columbia

By Isabel Nanton with Nancy Flight,
Barbara Tomlin, Yvonne Van Ruskenveld and
Lois Richardson, Editors

Consultants

Desmond Morton, FRSC, Professor of History,
University of Toronto

Jean Barman, Ed. D., Department of Social and Educational Studies,
University of British Columbia

Alan McMillan, Department of Social Sciences,
Douglas College, and Department of Archaeology,
Simon Fraser University

Grolier Limited
TORONTO

Downtown Vancouver seen from the south side of False Creek
Overleaf: Long Beach, Pacific Rim National Park, Vancouver Island

Canadian Cataloguing in Publication Data

Nanton, Isabel, 1951-
    British Columbia

(Discover Canada)
Includes index.
ISBN 0-7172-2716-2

1. British Columbia — Juvenile literature.
I. Flight, Nancy. II. Title. III. Series: Discover
Canada (Toronto, Ont.)

FC3811.2.N35 1994   971.1   C94-930922-2
F1087.4.N35 1994

Printed and bound in Canada.
Published simultaneously in the United States.
1 2 3 4 5 6 7 8 9 10   DWF   99 98 97 96 95

Front cover: North head of Ellerslie Lake, near
Bella Bella
Back cover: Totem pole at 'Ksan, a recreated
Gitksan village near Hazelton

The sunken Butchart Gardens, outside Victoria, have been planned to bloom year-round.

Table of Contents

CHAPTER 1

Land of Promise

Leonard George, chief of the Burrard Native Band, has said, "If there is still an Eden in the world, it would be British Columbia." Other people have referred to British Columbia as paradise or the Promised Land. Perhaps you have heard another well-known nickname for the province — Lotusland. All of these names reflect the special quality that has attracted many people to British Columbia.

The spectacular natural beauty of the province is one feature that makes British Columbia seem like Eden or paradise. Snow-capped mountains, deep blue fjords and inlets, lush rain forests, picturesque lakes and orchards, rolling grasslands and rushing rivers are all part of British Columbia's breathtaking landscape.

The richness of the land and its natural resources has generally provided a good life for the people of British Columbia. The Native peoples harvested salmon from the sea, built houses and totem poles out of cedar, made clothing from cedar bark and caught sea otters and other fur-bearing animals to trade for European goods. Later, people mined gold and other minerals from the earth. Today the B.C. economy still depends heavily on resource-based industries such as forestry, fishing and mining.

British Columbia is also a place where new ideas are welcome, where people can express their individuality and where there is plenty of economic opportunity. As a result, people from other parts of Canada and from nearly every country in the world have moved to British Columbia. Today a rich mosaic of people from many cultural backgrounds live in this land of promise by the Pacific.

The giant Douglas firs of Cathedral Grove in Vancouver Island's MacMillan Provincial Park

CHAPTER 2

The Land

British Columbia is Canada's third-largest province and covers an area of 948 600 square kilometres (366 280 square miles), or 9.5 percent of Canada's land area. It is nearly four times larger than Great Britain, two and a half times larger than Japan and larger than any American state except Alaska. From the beaches of the Pacific Ocean to the rocky peaks of its many mountain ranges, British Columbia is famous around the world for natural beauty.

Taking Shape

The huge mountains and deep valleys of British Columbia's landscape look solid and ancient, but the forces that created them are still at work beneath the earth's surface.

The rocks of British Columbia are not part of the original ancient continent of North America. They are separate huge chunks of rock originating far to the west and south that were pushed up against the continent millions of years ago by the forces of plate tectonics. According to the theory of plate tectonics, the earth's crust is broken up into huge plates that slowly move across the planet. Sometimes plates collide. As one plate pushes against another, the force of the collision can crumple solid rock, pushing it upwards to form mountains. British Columbia lies where plates meet. Some of its mountains are still being pushed up — the St. Elias Mountains in the northwest corner of the province are moving upwards at a rate of about four centimetres (1.6 inches) per year.

When two plates collide, they do not stop moving. One plate

Overleaf: **Alpine meadow in the Selkirk Mountains of southeastern British Columbia**

Above left: Fjord near Desolation Sound, one of many inlets that cut deep into the B.C. coastline. *Above right:* The Spectrum Range is part of a belt of volcanoes and lava plateaus that stretches from northwestern B.C. into the Yukon. *Left:* Monarch Ice Fields in the Coast Mountains, near Tweedsmuir Provincial Park

is forced under the other, sometimes causing earthquakes. British Columbia has the highest risk of earthquakes in Canada.

As a plate is pushed deeper into the earth, it gradually melts, and some of the magma finds it way to the surface, creating volcanoes. British Columbia has many volcanoes. None has erupted recently, but Native legends describe an eruption 200 years ago in the northwestern part of the province.

British Columbia's landscape has also been shaped by the grinding force of huge glaciers. During many ice ages, glaciers advanced and retreated, gouging out large valleys and carving out the coastal fjords that cut in from the Pacific Ocean.

Today you can still see remnants of the ice ages as small glaciers glisten in the sun on the tops of some of the province's tallest mountains.

Topography

British Columbia can be divided into four main topographical areas: the coastal area, the interior, the Rocky Mountains and the northern lowland.

The coastal area contains some of the province's most rugged landscape, in its mountains, and some of its gentlest, in the Fraser Valley. The Coast Mountains, the highest in North America, stretch northwest from Vancouver in a 1440-kilometre (895-mile) arc about 160 kilometres (100 miles) wide. The highest peak completely in the province is in the Coast Mountains: Mount Waddington at 4016 metres (13 175 feet).

The only flat part of the coastal area is in the south, where most of the population of British Columbia lives. The lower mainland, as it is known, contains the province's largest city, Vancouver, as well as the delta of the Fraser River, a rich farming area.

The coastal area also includes many islands. The largest are Vancouver Island and the Queen Charlotte Islands. They too are part of a mountain range, which continues into the far north of the province. On the mainland, this mountain range is the St. Elias Mountains. One of its peaks, Fairweather Mountain, right on the Alaska border, is the highest point in the province at 4663 metres (15 300 feet).

The islands and island groups off British Columbia's coast form a shield against the wind and waves of the open Pacific Ocean. They create the sheltered "Inside Passage" used by tugs with log booms, ferries, fishing boats, pleasure craft and other boat traffic.

The B.C. interior is a region of plateaus, valleys and mountain ranges. This varied area includes the snow-capped peaks of the Cassiar, Omineca, Monashee, Purcell and Selkirk mountain ranges as well as the rolling grasslands of the Cariboo-Chilcotin. The southern interior valley of the Okanagan contains a semi-desert complete with cacti and rattlesnakes.

The dividing line between the interior and the Rocky Mountains is the Rocky Mountain Trench. This huge valley, 3 to 20 kilometres (2 to 12 miles) wide, extends from Montana in the United States to the Yukon border. It was formed by faulting and erosion over millions of years.

The Rocky Mountains are the best-known mountains in Canada. They extend 1200 kilometres (745 miles) from the border with the United States almost to the Yukon. Along part of that distance, they form the border between British Columbia and Alberta. They also form part of a natural boundary known as the continental divide. This is the dividing line between North America's watersheds, where some rivers flow west to the Pacific Ocean, others flow north to the Arctic and still others flow east to empty eventually into the

Below left: **Mount Robson, the highest peak in the Canadian Rockies**
Below right: **The semi-desert lands of the southern Okanagan**

Atlantic Ocean. The highest peak in the Rockies is Mount Robson at 3977 metres (13 048 feet).

The northeastern corner of British Columbia, which lies east of the Rockies, is an extension of the high plains of western Alberta. Although it is part of the plains, this lowland is not completely flat. There are low, flat-topped hills and wide valleys. The Peace River flows through the southern part of the area, and the whole region is often called the Peace River Lowland.

Water

Thousands of lakes, rivers and streams shape British Columbia's landscape by erosion and deposition, but the landscape also strongly affects the shape and direction of the waterways.

A map of the province shows that most of the large lakes, such as Okanagan Lake in the south and Babine Lake farther north, are long and narrow. They lie in valleys formed by the many mountain ranges and plateaus. Most of the major rivers flow in a generally

Right: The clear waters of the Thompson River (right) disappear into the muddy, silt-laden Fraser near Lytton. *Far right:* Glacier-fed Takakkaw Falls plunges 254 metres (833 feet) into the Yoho River in Yoho National Park.

north-south direction for much of their route — following the valleys between the mountain ranges. Only three major rivers have found a way through the Coast Mountains to the Pacific Ocean: the Fraser, Skeena and Stikine. All three are important salmon rivers.

The Fraser River is the major river in British Columbia as it drains about one-quarter of the total area of the province. It rises as a tiny, clear trickle in the southeast corner of Mount Robson Park in the Rockies. Gathering silt and debris, it empties as a massive waterway 1280 kilometres (795 miles) later in the Pacific Ocean at Vancouver. Over millions of years, the Fraser has cut deep into the interior plateau and created a spectacular canyon. At Hell's Gate, the river rushes through canyon walls 1000 metres (3300 feet) high.

In the southeast corner of the province, the Columbia River flows north from its headwaters through the Rocky Mountain Trench. It turns sharply south at the north end of the Selkirk Mountain range and flows down into the United States. Many dams have been built along the Columbia both to control flooding and to produce hydroelectric power.

The biggest lakes in the province are the Williston and Nechako reservoirs that were created by damming rivers for hydroelectricity. Williston Lake covers 1660 square kilometres (640 square miles). British Columbia also has many natural lakes. Babine Lake is the largest one, covering 497 square kilometres (192 square miles).

Climate

British Columbia's climate is as varied as its landscape. Often areas separated by just a mountain range or a lake experience completely different climates. For example, the west coast of Vancouver Island is very wet. Over 250 centimetres (98 inches) of rain fall here annually, so a lush rain forest thrives. Yet the Gulf Islands in the Strait of Georgia on the opposite side of Vancouver Island lie in a rainshadow. On average, the yearly rainfall is only 80 centimetres (31 inches). Cacti grow there in the warm climate.

People living in the southern coastal zones and the southern Fraser River Valley enjoy Canada's longest frost-free period — over 200 days a year. This means that the last spring frosts occur in early April and the first fall frosts occur after Halloween.

The interior of the province is drier and hotter than the coast in summer and colder in the winter. The Okanagan Valley records an average of 2000 hours of sunshine each year. The long hours of sunshine and high summer temperatures have made the Okanagan one of Canada's major fruit-growing regions. Farther north, winters can be very harsh. The settlement of Smith River has recorded temperatures as low as -58.9 °C (-74 °F), and early morning frosts are common by the second week in August.

The northeast lowland has long, cold winters like the rest of the western plains. However, summers here are hot, and the frost-free period is long enough to grow grain, forage and other crops.

Below left: Irrigated farmlands in the Okanagan Valley, near Vernon. *Below right:* Autumn colours along the Peace River. *Right:* Winter near Fairmont Hotsprings in the Columbia Valley

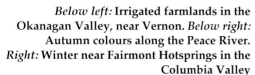

Wildlife

From ocean to mountaintop and rain forest to desert, British Columbia's many habitats are home to hundreds of species of animals. Because the Coast Mountains have acted as a barrier, some of these animals have developed differently from their relatives east of the mountains. The coastal blacktail deer, for instance, is a smaller version of the mule deer common elsewhere, and coastal black bears are larger than those found inland.

The largest animals in British Columbia are the whales. Passengers on the ferries between Vancouver and Victoria sometimes see orcas swimming by in large family groups called "pods," and grey whales migrate every year on a route along the west coast of Vancouver Island. Other mammals that inhabit these waters include sea otters, harbour seals and sea lions.

The five species of salmon found in B.C. waters are important food for both animals and humans. Pink, chum, coho, chinook and

Left: Orcas in Queen Charlotte Strait. *Bottom left:* Sea lions in Kyuquot Sound on the west coast of Vancouver Island. *Below:* Spawning sockeye salmon in the Adams River

sockeye salmon all live as adults in the open ocean but migrate inland along streams and rivers to lay their eggs in fresh water. Halibut and herring are also fished commercially.

The best place to see the small animals that live in the ocean's intertidal zone (between low and high tides) is in tidal pools on the rocky Pacific shore. There you might find sea anemones, starfish, sea urchins, snails, mussels and tiny crabs. On a sandy beach, you might find sand dollars.

On land, the British Columbia wilderness is home to large carnivores such as the grizzly bear, the cougar and the wolf. Members of the deer family, including the large wapiti (elk), are plentiful. Caribou live mainly in the northern part of the province, and mountain goats and bighorn sheep are common in mountainous areas. Moose browse along interior lakes and black bears roam the forests. Besides the cougar, two other wild cats are native to British Columbia: the lynx and the bobcat.

Smaller mammals include squirrels, chipmunks, badgers, rabbits, porcupines, raccoons, fishers, marmots and pikas. Amphibians and reptiles, such as Pacific tree frogs, rattlesnakes and alligator lizards, add to the large number of animal species that live in the province.

In the lakes, rivers and streams swim several kinds of trout, such as rainbow, brown, cutthroat, steelhead, and their relatives the Dolly Varden and lake trout. Squawfish and carp are very common, but less well known than the trout and char. While sea-going salmon return to fresh waters to spawn, one type of salmon, the kokanee, is landlocked — it never leaves its lake environment.

British Columbia's many species of birds add sound and colour to wilderness, farmland, towns and cities. Albatrosses, puffins, cormorants, oystercatchers and gulls are just some of the seabirds that live along the coast. Ducks are abundant throughout the province. The great blue heron picks its way cautiously through shallow waters, both salt and fresh. Birds of prey range in size from golden and bald eagles with wingspans of almost two metres (6.6 feet) to the tiny pygmy owl, which may weigh as little as 50 grams

Far left: **The white Kermode bear, found only on Princess Royal Island and a small stretch of coastal B.C. south of Prince Rupert, is really a very rare colour variation of black bear. The two bears seen here are brother and sister.**
Top left: **A family of mountain goats, barely visible as they make their sure-footed way along a rocky slope.**
Bottom left: **Tufted puffins**

(two ounces). The smallest birds in the province are the tiny hummingbirds that arrive early each spring from their winter homes in Mexico.

The mouth of the Fraser River is especially important to migrating waterfowl and shorebirds. Millions of them stop here during their spring and fall migrations, including thousands of snowgeese from Siberia.

Forests

Forests cover almost two-thirds of British Columbia. On the wet west coast are the huge trees of the temperate rain forest. The gentle climate, long growing season, fertile soil and large amount of rain allow some trees here to grow more than 90 metres (295 feet) tall. Some of these huge trees are over 1000 years old.

The main rain forest trees are western red cedar, western hemlock, amabilis and Douglas firs and Sitka spruce. They grow in a very limited area: no more than about 80 kilometres (50 miles) inland and no higher than about 300 metres (985 feet) above sea level.

Also on the coast are the dry coastal woodlands of southeastern Vancouver Island, the Gulf Islands and the extreme south of the Fraser Valley. Forests in this area contain a mix of coniferous and deciduous trees. While Douglas fir and lodgepole pine are plentiful, so are Garry oak and alder. Canada's only broad-leaved evergreen, the arbutus, grows here.

East of the Coast Mountains, the forests of the interior reflect a variety of climates from the dry, hot grasslands to the wetter, western-facing mountain slopes. The semi-desert grasslands are not heavily forested, but treed areas are common. The trees here include ponderosa pine, Douglas fir, juniper, birch, trembling aspen and chokecherry. Similar trees are found in the dry montane forests of the plateaus and on lower slopes of mountains. Higher still are the subalpine forests that include spruce, mountain hemlock, alpine fir, lodgepole pine, alpine larch, whitebark pine and trembling aspen. Westward-facing mountain slopes receive more rain than the rest of the interior because they catch the moisture-laden clouds moving east from the Pacific Ocean. On these slopes, western red cedar, western hemlock, Douglas fir, western larch, spruce, yew and bitter cherry grow.

The boreal forest that covers most of the rest of Canada with a mix of conifers, birches and poplars is only found in the northern parts of British Columbia.

Wildflowers

In the densest, darkest part of the rain forest, few wildflowers grow, but elsewhere in British Columbia, flowers and other plants thrive. The mild climate of southwestern British Columbia brings flowers out early: even in January several species of wildflowers may bloom on Vancouver Island and the Gulf Islands. In these dry coastal woodlands, flowers such as blue camas, chocolate lily, shooting star and sea blush colour the landscape.

Some of the most spectacular displays of wildflowers are seen on high alpine meadows. Here the growing season may be as short as 25 days, and summer blizzards can occur. Plants must grow quickly. Lupines, paintbrushes, daisies, western anemones and columbines are just some of the flowers that brighten these meadows during the short summer.

Deep in the forest of Carmanah Pacific Park. *Inset left:* **Glacier lilies in the Cascade Mountains.** *Inset right:* **Along with the trees that are native to the province are apple and other fruit trees that now thrive in irrigated areas of the Okanagan Valley.**

CHAPTER 3

The People

People have come from all over the world to live in British Columbia. Over the past 200 years or so, they have come from 140 countries and from other parts of Canada.

For thousands of years before that, the area's first inhabitants, the Native people, lived on the abundant natural resources of the coast and the interior. Experts estimate that there were more than 80 000 Native people in the land that became British Columbia when the first Europeans arrived.

First Nations

In the beginning, an ocean covered all of the earth. Then Raven created an island. Plants, animals and the first people appeared on the island. People and animals could talk to each other and change what they looked like. Over time, Raven transformed the people, animals and landscape into what they are today.

This is the story of creation that is told by some of the Native people living on the coast of British Columbia. They believe they have always lived there. Modern archaeologists agree that Native people have occupied what is now British Columbia for a very long time — 10 000 to 12 000 years.

The people lived in groups that were very different from each other. Thirty-four different languages were spoken. Some groups traded with each other; others fought wars with each other. Today, these groups are called First Nations because they were here first — before Europeans came.

British Columbians at work and play

Coastal Nations

From north to south, the Native nations living on the coast were the Tlingit, Tsimshian, Haida, Bella Coola, Kwakiutl, Nootka, and Coast Salish. Within some of these groups were smaller groups that spoke different, though closely related, languages.

Each nation had its own culture and traditions, but each also held some things in common. Many had a class system that included nobles, commoners and slaves captured in wars. Marriages were usually arranged to unite families. On the north coast, women held more important positions than on the south coast. Among the Haida on Haida Gwaii (the Queen Charlotte Islands), families traced their ancestry through the mother, and women sometimes became chiefs.

The Native people believed that everyone had a soul, which still lived after the person died. They believed that certain men or women, called shamans, had the power to heal those who were sick or had lost their soul. If too many of a shaman's patients died, the shaman might be killed by the villagers.

The coastal economy was based on the sea and the forests. Seals, salmon, halibut, mussels, clams, herring roe and seaweed provided food and trade items. So many shellfish were eaten that all along the coast today you can see large mounds of discarded

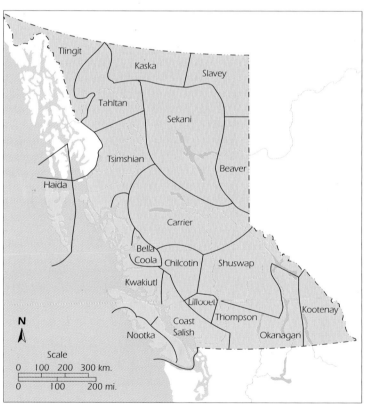

This map shows the areas occupied by the main Native groups when the first Europeans arrived.

24

shells that piled up over the centuries. The Nootka, on the west coast of Vancouver Island, also hunted whales in their eight-person canoes. And every spring, the Tsimshian set up camp at the mouth of the Nass River to catch the small, oily eulachon or candlefish that came there in huge numbers to spawn. Eulachon oil, extracted by cooking the fish in wooden vats, was used as a buttery sauce and a berry preservative. Tsimshian traders carried it in wooden boxes along "grease trails," well-used paths to the interior. The trails included bridges and canoe routes.

All Native people had great respect for the land and the animals. The coastal nations believed that salmon were people who had eternal life and lived in a large house deep in the ocean. Every spring these people took on the form of salmon and gave themselves to humans for food. After the Native people ate salmon, they put the bones in the water to wash out to sea and change again into salmon people.

During the summer, men fished and women gathered berries and plants for food. Most of the winter was spent indoors in large

Left: The interior of a Coast Salish house, by Paul Kane. Coast Salish women were skilled weavers who made beautiful blankets from spun mountain goat wool and dog hair. *Below:* Traditional houses and totem poles at 'Ksan, a reconstructed Gitksan village near Hazelton. The Gitksan are one of the three Tsimshian peoples (the Nishga and the Coast Tsimshian are the others).

"longhouses" that might hold ten families, each with its own living area. The houses were made of planks that were split from cedar logs and fitted into a frame of cedar posts. The posts and walls were often decorated with carvings and paintings. Sleeping benches were built along the outer walls. Cedar mats and wooden storage boxes were used as walls to divide the living areas. Fish were hung to dry on racks hanging from the ceiling.

During the cold, rainy winter, the adults and children gathered around a large central fire to tell stories or play games. The men built canoes and tools and carved masks, and the women wove baskets and clothing from strips of bark and roots.

Carved totem poles representing family histories or Native legends were often placed at the front of a house. Ravens, eagles, whales, bears, beavers, mythical beings and human figures were carved on the poles. Some poles were raised as a memorial when an important person died or when someone became a chief.

When a new totem pole was raised, a potlatch was usually planned. The potlatch was like a big party held to celebrate important events such as a marriage or a newly built house or a new chief taking power. Sometimes the potlatch just celebrated a family's high status.

Guests came to the potlatch from many villages. They sometimes stayed for days, feasting, dancing, singing and telling stories about their history. The host gave many valuable gifts to all the guests. The gifts included beautifully carved canoes, masks and bowls, skins, fishing rights and even slaves. To show their wealth, everyone tried to give more and better gifts than others had given.

Interior Nations

Native nations living in the interior were the Interior Salish, which includes the Okanagan, Lillooet, Thompson and Shuswap peoples; the Athapaskan, which includes the Chilcotin, Carrier, Sekani, Tahltan, Kaska, Slavey and Beaver peoples; and the Kootenay.

Life in the interior was harder than on the coast. The weather was

Far left: In winter, the Interior Salish lived in pit-houses called *kikulis.*
Left: The distinctive shape of Kootenay bark canoes — with pointy ends that extended underwater — was well suited to the rushing rivers of the B.C. interior.

harsher, and it took more effort to find food. People moved around more — they were nomadic. Because of this, they did not have as many possessions as coastal Natives did, and there was more equality among people.

Some interior groups lived beside rivers where they could catch salmon, which came far upstream to spawn. Other groups often spent the summer near lakes and streams where they could fish, but they depended primarily on hunting for food.

All interior groups hunted, even during the snowy winters, using spears or bows and arrows to kill large animals, such as deer and elk, and snares made of rope to catch groundhogs, rabbits and other small animals. They also gathered berries and edible roots.

As on the coast, Native people living in the interior respected the spirits of the fish and animals they killed. For example, when the Athapaskan killed a bear for its meat and fur, they apologized to it and honoured it by placing its skull in the fork of a tree.

Some people, such as the Kootenay, lived in lodges made from buffalo hides that could be taken down easily and moved. In winter, the Interior Salish lived in *kikulis*. The bottom half of these dwellings were pits dug into the earth, which provided good insulation from the cold. The dome-shaped roof was made of logs and poles that were covered by soil. Several families might live together in a kikuli.

The Native peoples of the interior traded such things as mountain goat skins, lichen dyes, obsidian and soapberries for dried seaweed, shells and eulachon oil from the coast.

Contact with Europeans

Europeans began exploring the coast of British Columbia in the late 1700s. First to come were Spaniards from Mexico, then came the British, who soon established a profitable trade in sea otter furs with China. In the early 1800s, the British also began coming into British Columbia by land from the east to set up fur-trading posts.

After the arrival of Europeans, the trading activities of the Native people changed. The newcomers wanted furs, and so Native people hunted otter and trapped beaver to trade for blankets, buttons, iron and other items they could barter from the Europeans. They were sharp traders and were said to check the quality of European trade goods carefully and reject inferior items.

The fur trade did not do much to change the culture of the Native people other than to increase the wealth of some groups. The European traders, especially those who came overland from the east or south, depended on help from Native people, who shared food and housing with them and guided them over the mountains. Some Native women married Europeans.

New Settlers

Fur traders came and went, but few people settled in British Columbia. By 1855, only about 500 non-Natives lived around Fort Victoria on Vancouver Island, and another 150 around Nanaimo. There were even fewer settlers on the mainland.

Some Black immigrants became policemen in Victoria and later formed a militia unit, the Victoria Pioneer Rifle Company. For a time, this was the only organized defence force in the colony.

All this changed with the gold rush, which began in 1858. More than 30 000 Americans, Chinese and Europeans streamed into British Columbia over the next few years. Most came looking for gold in the Fraser River near Hope and later in the Cariboo, but others came to supply goods and services to the gold-seekers. Among the Americans who came were a large number of Black men and women who had left California because of racial discrimination. A few of them headed for the gold fields, but most settled around Fort Victoria and on Saltspring Island, where they farmed, started businesses and worked in a variety of jobs. Many, but by no means all, returned to the United States after the American Civil War.

Most of the gold and the gold-seekers were gone by 1866, but many of the new people stayed on. They began farming on Vancouver Island and in the Lower Fraser Valley. They raised cattle in the Cariboo and hunted whales and seals off the coast of Vancouver Island. They mined coal on Vancouver Island, and they logged the giant trees in the coastal forests.

The next great influx of settlers came after British Columbia joined Confederation, when construction finally began on the promised railway that would link it to the rest of Canada.

Building the railway through British Columbia was an enormous job. Chinese labourers were brought from China and San Francisco

Vancouver's Chinatown at the turn of the century and today

to help with the work. In the early 1880s, about 4000 Chinese lived in British Columbia. By the early 1890s, after the railway was built, the Chinese population had doubled.

During the same period, the European population more than tripled. Most of these new arrivals came from other parts of Canada, especially Ontario and the Maritimes. They came because farm land and jobs were available. Japanese people also began coming to British Columbia in the 1880s, mainly to fish, and Sikhs came from India to work in logging camps and sawmills.

Among the new settlers, most of the adults were men. In some areas in the interior, men outnumbered women by ten to one. Among the Native people, the number of men and women was more equal, but the entire Native population was declining.

Conflict of Cultures

After gold was discovered and settlers began to move into the area, conflict developed between the Native people and the newcomers. The Europeans wanted to own land to farm and to build houses on. Native people did not believe anyone could own the sacred land — they just travelled over it.

The Europeans began to take the land, without treaties and

without adequate compensation, and made laws that forced the Native people to live only in certain areas called reserves. Some Native peoples, such as the Nishga living in the Nass Valley, protested. In 1888, when the government wanted to give them a piece of land to live on, a Nishga spokesperson said, "How can they give it when it is our own.... They have never bought it from us or our forefathers. They have never fought or conquered our people.... It has been ours for thousands of years...."

There were other problems, too. The Native people had no immunity to European diseases, and many thousands died of smallpox, measles and tuberculosis spread by Europeans.

The Canadian government wanted the Native people to live like Europeans. The potlatch was outlawed. Laws were passed to control the way Natives fished. Native children were forced to live in schools run by Europeans, where they were not allowed to speak their own languages, but had to speak English. Missionaries taught them Christianity.

The Twentieth Century

By 1901, for the first time, the majority of the people living in British Columbia were of British heritage. Almost 11 percent of the population were people of Asian heritage, the same as today.

More and more British moved to British Columbia, attracted by the mild climate, the jobs in resource industries, such as forestry and mining, and the hunting and fishing. The province was so British, in fact, that people drove on the left side. One visitor wrote that a person from Ontario would not feel at home in Vancouver.

Meanwhile, people from other countries continued to immigrate. Scandinavians, Greeks, Italians and Basques built their own communities. Doukhobors, a Christian group originally from Russia, moved to British Columbia from Saskatchewan. They bought land as a group in the Kootenays and remain there today.

The Doukhobors and the Mennonites, another religious group

In the 1920s, Japanese British Columbians put together their own baseball team, the Vancouver Asahis. It was one of the best baseball teams of the twenties and thirties.

from Europe, tried to stay apart from other British Columbians. They wanted to live according to their religion and not according to Canadian ways. Other newcomers wanted to be part of Canadian life, but sometimes were not allowed to be. Asians, in particular, suffered many forms of discrimination during the first half of the century.

After the Second World War, many Europeans came to British Columbia looking for a better life. They came from Italy, Germany, Portugal, Czechoslovakia, Ukraine and Holland. Later political upheavals around the world brought many more immigrants to the province — from Hungary in the mid-1950s (all the teachers and students from one Hungarian forestry school came as a group to UBC); from India, Pakistan and Tibet in the 1960s and 1970s; from Vietnam and Cambodia in the 1970s and 1980s; from Hong Kong after 1984, the year the British agreed to return Hong Kong to Chinese rule in 1997.

In the 1960s and 1970s, another group of newcomers made an impact on British Columbia. Thousands of young people from other parts of Canada and from the United States moved here. Many stayed in Vancouver, but others settled in the Gulf Islands, the Kootenays, and the Shuswap lakes to live simply in the country.

In the past few decades, the province has also welcomed immigrants from Korea, Thailand, Uganda, Latin America, South Africa and the Caribbean. Very recently, people from Romania and from the former East Germany and Yugoslavia have made their way to British Columbia.

British Columbia has welcomed many new groups of immigrants in recent decades.

Native Rebirth

During the early and middle 1900s, many Native people in British Columbia suffered from the destruction of their way of life. They were not allowed to follow their own customs and faced discrimination when they tried to live away from the reserves. On reserves, many bands lived with constant unemployment, poverty, alcoholism and family problems. Their numbers continued to decline — in 1929, the total Native population was only 22 605.

Then the long downward trend reversed itself. By 1950, there were almost 30 000 Native people living in the province. At the end of 1992, there were over 90 000.

Left: Master carver Charles Edenshaw (c. 1839-1920) was one of the first Haida artists to gain widespread recognition. *Above:* Argillite carving is a specialty of Haida artists as the beautiful soft stone is found only in the mountains of southern Graham Island.

In recent years, the First Nations have been asserting their rights. In 1982, "existing aboriginal rights" were recognized by the Canadian Constitution. Native people began talking about returning to Native self-government. They have filed "land claims" to reclaim ownership rights to their land. They have led protests against the government. They have found new pride in their history, traditions and art. Native artists are now famous throughout the world for their prints, masks, sculpture and modern totem poles.

Today's People

Today, about three and a half million people live in British Columbia. Fewer than half the non-Natives were born in the province. Some 30 percent moved here from other provinces, 20 percent from other countries. Although their numbers continue to grow, Native people are now only 2.69 percent of British Columbia's population, down from 100 percent barely two centuries ago. About half live on reserves all over the province.

People from other parts of Canada come to British Columbia for jobs, for the milder climate and for the mountains and the sea. Many come when they retire. People from other countries come to British Columbia to join their families, to flee persecution, to seek freedom or to enjoy a better life.

More than half of the province's people live in the Lower Mainland. It is still growing rapidly, especially in the suburban areas south of the city. The next largest population areas are around Victoria, Prince George, Kamloops, Kelowna and Nanaimo.

The cultural mix of people in British Columbia means that a number of different religions are practised here. Many aboriginal people are rediscovering their Native spiritual roots. Almost 75 percent of British Columbians today say they are Protestant. Nearly 15 percent are Roman Catholic. Among the others are Hindus, Muslims, Jews and Buddhists.

Just as Christians celebrate their special holidays of Christmas and Easter, British Columbia's other cultural and religious groups

A couple of today's citizens, and of tomorrow's

celebrate special days. Hindus and Sikhs celebrate Diwali, the festival of lights, with fireworks in the fall. The Chinese have colourful parades and dragon dances to celebrate their New Year in January or February. Jews celebrate their New Year, Rosh Hashanah, in early fall.

The Future

In the early 1990s, British Columbia was Canada's fastest-growing province. It will probably continue to attract people from other places.

From the time the first Europeans arrived, the First Nations have seen new groups moving in. The newcomers often wear different clothes, eat different food and speak different languages. This great variety among the people in British Columbia makes it an exciting and challenging place to live.

CHAPTER 4

Early Exploration and Settlement

During the 1700s, ships from many nations sailed the seas looking for new trade routes and new worlds to explore. A growing European population wanted more spices, silks, tea, gold, furs and fish. Fleets from Russia, Britain, Spain, France, Portugal and Holland competed with each other in an effort to claim new lands and obtain access to these and other resources.

First European Explorers

Russian interest in the Pacific Northwest began in the early 1700s and increased after Vitus Bering's 1740 expedition returned with several hundred sea otter pelts. The Spanish, who had claimed the entire Pacific coast in the sixteenth century, became concerned about this Russian presence in the north and dispatched ships from Mexico to establish Spain's sovereignty.

The first of three Spanish expeditions left from Mexico under Commander Juan Pérez Hernández and reached the Pacific Northwest in 1774. Hernández's ship, the *Santiago,* dropped anchor first off the Queen Charlotte Islands and then in Nootka Sound, halfway down the west coast of Vancouver Island. At both places, local Natives visited the Santiago and exchanged sea otter pelts for clothing, beads and knives. The next year, a Spanish ship commanded by Juan Francisco de la Bodega y Quadra travelled as far north as the Alaska Panhandle and erected a large wooden cross to claim the coast for Spain. After a third voyage in 1779, the Spanish felt confident that their claim to the area was well established.

Captain James Cook at Nootka Sound, April 1778

Captain James Cook

In 1776, Captain James Cook left Britain in search of the Northwest Passage — a sea route from Europe to the Orient that many people believed would be found through North American waters. British ships had been searching for this route for more than 200 years when Cook was sent to look for the passage from the Pacific side.

After voyaging through the South Sea islands, Cook reached Nootka Sound in 1778. Thirty canoes filled with Nootka people greeted his ships. The Nootka chief, Maquinna, waved a bird-shaped rattle in formal welcome and scattered eagle down on the water. Cook and his crew stayed for four weeks, repairing their ships and brewing up enough spruce beer to prevent scurvy on their onward journey. After sailing farther north without finding a passage, the expedition travelled south to the Sandwich Islands (now known as Hawaii) to pass the winter. Cook died in the islands in 1779, but his crew continued on to China as planned. There the sea otter pelts obtained for next to nothing from the Native people were sold for large sums of money. While the expedition did not succeed in finding the Northwest Passage, it did succeed in starting a fur trade that lasted for the next 50 years and in establishing Britain's presence in the area.

Captain George Vancouver

The maritime trade in sea otter pelts that grew up after Cook's expedition led to the arrival of many explorers and mapmakers. In 1792, Captain George Vancouver travelled from England and began the job of surveying and charting the coastline. At Nootka Sound he met the Spanish commander Bodega y Quadra. Although their countries were involved in a dispute over control of the area, the two became friends. In fact, Vancouver named the land where he had met the Spanish commander "Quadra's and Vancouver's Island." (Mapmakers later shortened it to "Vancouver Island.")

Vancouver explored the area over the course of three summers, mapping much of the coastline and naming many places.

Captain George Vancouver and his survey team off the B.C. coast. Vancouver first visited the area as a young midshipman with Cook's expedition. He is now considered to have been one of the world's great navigators and mapmakers.

Alexander Mackenzie

While Vancouver and Quadra were surveying the Pacific coast, other explorers were charting routes down rivers and through the mountains. One of them was Alexander Mackenzie, the first of the Pacific Northwest's great fur-trader explorers.

Mackenzie began working in the fur trade when he was 15 years old. He was 25 and a partner in the North West Company when he began looking for a canoe route from Lake Athabasca to the Pacific Ocean. In his first attempt he travelled down the river that now bears his name and reached the Arctic Ocean. In his second attempt, he travelled down the Peace and Fraser rivers.

Mackenzie's second great exploration, like his first, depended on the strength of voyageur paddlers and the skills and knowledge of Native guides and interpreters. On the journey to the Pacific, his party paddled through narrow canyons and dragged heavy canoes up hill sides. Struggling over many obstacles, the group crossed the Rocky Mountains and the interior plateau, then followed the centuries-old Grease Trail, used by Native people to transport eulachon oil into the interior.

In 1793, Mackenzie finally reached salt water at Bella Coola, the first European to travel overland to the Pacific. On his arrival, he used a mixture of vermilion and melted grease to record his achievement on a rock just above the tide line.

Simon Fraser

Simon Fraser, another of the Pacific Northwest's fur-trader explorers, joined the North West Company at age 16 and was 29 when he was put in charge of fur-trading operations in the area now

Right: Simon Fraser and his party at Hell's Gate. Fraser later wrote of the experience in his diary: "I have been for a long period among the Rocky Montains, but have never seen anything to equal this country, for I cannot find words to describe our situation at times. We had to pass where no human being should venture." *Below:* Mackenzie's inscription. Rain eventually washed the words away, but in 1926 the Historic Sites and Monuments Board had them carved in the rock and filled with red cement.

known as central British Columbia. After building four trading posts in the area, Fraser tried to find a safe canoe route to the Pacific Ocean. Accompanied by 19 voyageurs, and ignoring the advice of Native people, Fraser set out in 1808 to travel down the river that now bears his name. Shooting through rapids and whirlpools, the members of Fraser's group navigated treacherous waters until they were forced to abandon their canoes at the narrow gorge known as Hell's Gate. There they had to drag their baggage over a faint trail that ran along a sheer rock wall high above rushing waters. Supplies ran out after this and everyone had to eat berries and moss. Yet the expedition members survived, and after they obtained some canoes from Native people, they continued on to the coast.

Even though the river travelled by Fraser never became a useful fur-trade route, it did become an important travel "corridor." Almost 200 years after Simon Fraser's journey, people are still travelling by road and by rail along the banks of the Fraser River.

David Thompson

While Simon Fraser was looking for a canoe route to the Pacific, British-born David Thompson was exploring the Rocky Mountains in search of another possible canoe route. Like both Fraser and Mackenzie, Thompson entered the fur trade as a young man. He began working for the Hudson's Bay Company (HBC) when he was 14. After learning the skills of a surveyor, Thompson left the HBC to work for the rival North West Company. He soon became its leading mapmaker.

In 1807, Thompson followed the Columbia River to Lake Windermere and constructed a trading fort. Using the fort as a base, he continued to explore and map the area that is now southeastern British Columbia. Often his Métis wife and their three small children travelled with him.

Thompson finally reached the mouth of the Columbia River in 1811, but he was too late to claim the territory for Britain — Americans had already arrived and built a fort. Today Thompson is remembered for his accurate maps and the colourful journals he wrote about his explorations.

The Fur Trade

As the newly charted riverways opened up the West, the land-based fur trade expanded, and competition intensified between the North West and Hudson's Bay companies.

The Montreal-based North West Company controlled trade in the area now known as British Columbia through a network of forts that included Fort St. James, Fort Fraser, Fort George, Fort Kamloops and Kootenay House. The Hudson's Bay Company was a powerful firm based in England and, until 1820, had no forts west of the Rocky Mountains. In 1821, the two companies finally realized that competition was ruining them both and agreed to merge under the name of the Hudson's Bay Company.

The 20 years after the merger were relatively stable ones. The HBC's governor in North America, George Simpson, worked to make the company more powerful and more efficient. In 1841, Simpson decided to move the company's west coast headquarters from Fort Vancouver on the Columbia River to Vancouver Island. He sent HBC Chief Factor James Douglas to choose a suitable location, and in 1843 the construction of Fort Victoria began in a cove on the southern tip of Vancouver Island.

But even before Fort Victoria was finished, the fur trade in the Pacific Northwest had started to change. Some fur-bearing animals were declining in numbers, and ownership of the area west of the Rocky Mountains was in dispute. Britain had granted the HBC trading rights over territories that extended as far south as present-day Oregon, but some American political leaders insisted that all the lands between California and Alaska belonged to the United States. There was even talk of war before the two parties reached an agreement in 1846 and signed a treaty that gave Britain all of Vancouver Island and established the border with the United States

James Douglas
supervises early
construction work
on Fort Victoria in
1843.

at the 49th parallel. The fur trade did not revive, however. European demand for furs lessened, and the trade that had once been a source of great wealth continued to decline.

The Native people who had been essential to the trade continued to feel the effects of the changes it brought them for many, many years. Traditional ways had been undermined, alcohol had disrupted community life, and diseases like smallpox and influenza had ravaged whole villages. Unfortunately, the decline of the fur trade did not mean the end of these problems.

As the heyday of the fur trade came to a close, the days of the settler began. The farming and fishing activity that had been carried on around forts in order to feed the traders increased as more settlers arrived. Then came an event that added impetus to the drive to settle the land west of the Rockies — the discovery of gold.

The Rush for Gold

In 1858, news of gold found on Fraser River sandbars reached San Francisco, and boats filled with miners streamed north to Victoria.

Within days, Victoria's population grew from a few hundred to thousands. A huge tent city sprang up to shelter an international community of gold-seekers: native-born Americans, Chinese, Germans, Italians, Spaniards and many others who had already tried their luck in the California gold fields.

The miners bought supplies and licences, then boarded a variety of vessels to cross Georgia Strait to the mainland. Some of the boats were no bigger and no safer than bathtubs, and many people drowned. The miners who reached the mainland then had to tramp through dense forest and over rugged mountains. Some of them were rewarded for their efforts — before the end of 1858 about $1.6 million worth of gold was taken from the stretch of river between Hope and Lillooet.

The arrival of more than 25 000 people during 1858 changed the sparsely populated mainland. Shanty towns grew up with the influx of miners and the arrival of innkeepers, builders and merchants who saw the possibility of profit in the Fraser River Gold Rush.

Since many of the miners in the new shanty towns came from the United States, there was renewed fear of American domination. James Douglas, who had been made governor of the Vancouver Island colony in 1849, was quick to let leaders in Britain know about this fear. When Britain decided to assert its authority by creating another colony on the mainland, Douglas was asked to take on a second governorship. In 1858, he became governor of the new colony of British Columbia.

The mainland government soon had a second gold rush to deal with. In 1862, a Cornishman named Billy Barker struck "paydirt" after digging a 13-metre (42-foot) shaft at Williams Creek near present-day Quesnel. Within two weeks a new town, Barkerville, had sprung up, with hotels, bakeries, blacksmith shops, stores, banks and even a theatre. Men made fortunes and then lost them as they drank, gambled and danced with the hurdy-gurdy girls. Billy Barker himself lost his fortune and died a pauper.

Above: For a time, Barkerville was the gold rush capital of the world. Much of it burned down in 1868, but by then the Cariboo Gold Rush was virtually over. *Left:* Camels were introduced as pack animals into the Cariboo in 1862. It no doubt seemed like a good idea, since camels could carry a lot more than a mule or a horse, but it turned out that their feet were unsuited to the rocky, muddy terrain.

The Fraser River and Cariboo gold rushes dramatically increased the populations of Vancouver Island and British Columbia. Prospectors of every nationality flocked to the two colonies. More people often meant more trouble. The man who helped Governor Douglas control lawlessness during and after the gold rush was the legendary Judge Matthew Baillie Begbie.

Judge Begbie almost singlehandedly upheld law and order from

Catherine Schubert was the only woman among a group of gold-seekers known as the Overlanders of '62, who travelled overland to the Cariboo from present-day Winnipeg. The trek through the mountains was harrowing for everyone, but especially for Mrs. Schubert, who gave birth to a daughter only a few hours after arriving in Kamloops. The baby, Rose, was the first non-Native child born in the B.C. interior.

New Westminster on the coast to the Cariboo gold fields. He was often seen riding on horseback as he travelled to every corner of the colony to hear trials in halls, tents and open fields. Between 1859 and 1872 he presided over 52 murder trials. Twenty-seven of the people found guilty by the juries were hanged.

As well as contributing to the establishment of a justice system, the gold rushes led to the development of new and better routes for transporting people and goods. In 1859, the Royal Engineers arrived and began the work of choosing sites for cities and ports, planning the layout of communities and building bridges and roads. The largest road-building project was a wagon route stretching north from Yale to the Cariboo. Under the command of Colonel Richard Moody, the Royal Engineers laid out a 650-kilometre (400-mile) route and did most of the dangerous rock-blasting work in the Fraser Canyon. The Cariboo Wagon Road was completed in 1865 and immediately made travel by ox-drawn wagon and stagecoach much easier. Settlers began using the road to reach homesteads and communities in the interior. Several of the "Mile Houses" that catered to travellers along the way can still be seen from the Trans-Canada Highway, which follows some of the route.

Becoming a Province

During the gold rush period, ranchers began raising cattle on the natural grasslands of the southern Cariboo, Catholic priests planted the first fruit orchards and grape vines in the Okanagan Valley, and

Building the Cariboo Road

Chinese settlers on Vancouver Island grew vegetables for local use. Soon land rather than gold began to attract people who saw the economic potential of farming, fishing and logging in the two colonies.

In the mid-1860s, British authorities decided that the development of Vancouver Island and British Columbia would be strengthened if they were united. Accordingly, in November 1866 the two colonies became the United Colony of British Columbia. The new colony had a 23-member legislative council with nine elected members, four from the island and five from the mainland. New Westminster became the first capital, but lost its position two years later when government officials voted to move the seat of government to Victoria.

One of the chief forces behind the move from New Westminster to Victoria was a man who stands first in a long line of colourful British Columbia politicians — Amor De Cosmos. Born in Nova

Scotia, William Alexander Smith was a journalist who travelled to the California gold fields and changed his name to Amor De Cosmos — "Lover of the Universe." After arriving in Victoria, the outspoken De Cosmos started the *British Colonist* newspaper and was soon deeply involved in politics.

De Cosmos was one of the most active promoters of union with the new Dominion of Canada. In 1867, the colonies of New Brunswick, Nova Scotia, and the United Province of Canada

Coaling station at Nanaimo, 1859. Even before the gold rush, the discovery of coal in the Nanaimo area was attracting miners to Vancouver Island. By the mid-1880s, coal would overtake gold as the province's most valuable mineral.

(Quebec and Ontario) had joined in a Canadian Confederation. Some British Columbians agreed with De Cosmos and wanted to become part of the Dominion; others thought the colony should join the United States. When the Dominion promised a transcontinental rail link, opponents to the plan were won over. In 1871, British Columbia entered Confederation with the assurance that a railway joining the province with the rest of the Dominion would be built by 1881.

Even with the promise of a rail link, the new province was far from strong. The decline of the fur trade and the end of the gold rush had left the economy in an uncertain state. The population of 40 000 consisted of almost 30 000 Native people and a mixture of Europeans, Chinese and Americans. In some areas there were hardly any non-Native women to share in the work of building and maintaining settlements. These settlements consisted of Native villages, some fur trade depots, fading gold-mining towns and a few well-established communities — all scattered across a large and rugged territory. The province builders had their work cut out for them.

Fort Street, Victoria, about the time of Confederation

CHAPTER 5
The Province Grows

W hen British Columbia entered Confederation on July 20, 1871, life was difficult for the fur traders, miners, merchants and settlers in the new province, but it was particularly difficult for the Native peoples of the region. Over one-third of the Native population had died during the smallpox epidemics of the early gold rush years. Those who survived soon faced an entirely different social, economic and political order. With the decline of the fur trade and the end of the gold rush came a push to clear and use the land in a way that was foreign to Native culture. Europeans lived by cultivating and building and settling on land, practices that were incompatible with the hunting and gathering traditions of Native peoples. Tension between the two groups increased. Although no treaties were signed, Native lands were reduced to small reserves. Discouraged by government (the potlatch would even be banned), Native traditions gave way to European ones, despite the fact that there were more Native people than Europeans living in British Columbia until well into the 1880s.

The Canadian Pacific Railway

After Confederation, fishers, miners, loggers and farmers had spread out across the province and settled close to the major transportation routes in an effort to use the province's resources and earn a living. Canneries were built all along the coast to process salmon caught in the major runs on the Fraser, Skeena and Nass rivers. Sawmills were built to turn trees into lumber, and crops were planted. The railway

Logging camp, Vancouver Island, in the early 1900s

Above: The Honourable Donald Smith, one of the founders of the Canadian Pacific Railway Company, drives in the ceremonial last spike symbolizing the completion of the railway from Halifax on the east coast to Port Moody on the west. *Right:* Chinese railway workers had their own separate camps, which were usually little more than a group of flimsy tents.

that colonists had been promised before Confederation was needed more than ever. The wagon roads, trails and riverways could not transport all the supplies required or the goods produced.

After many delays, the construction of the British Columbia portion of the Canadian Pacific Railway (CPR) finally began in 1880. The railway builders soon discovered that the province's rugged terrain made building a route to the coast a massive undertaking. Surveyors working in the Rocky Mountains studied several routes before choosing the Kicking Horse and Rogers passes. While looking for the pass that would later bear his name, CPR engineer Major A.B. Rogers and his surveyors ran into terrible weather and were forced to pitch their tents in the snow. Almost frozen, the men then had to beat each other with their pack straps to keep warm.

While the survey crews endured hardships, the construction crews suffered even more. Tunnelling through solid rock, balancing on half-built bridges over fast-moving water and living in cold and uncomfortable camps, many workers died from accidents and disease. Among the workers were over 15 000 Chinese labourers who were brought from China and San Francisco to blast railbeds and place ties. The hard work and the poor conditions in their segregated camps led to the death of at least 600 Chinese workers.

Despite delays and difficulties and the death of many workers, the railway was completed at last. On November 7, 1885, a crowd of CPR officials and railway workers gathered at Craigellachie in the Selkirk Mountains. There they watched as the "last spike" was driven in, and a railway joining British Columbia to Canada was finished.

Vancouver's Rise

The completion of the Canadian Pacific Railway had a direct effect on Coal Harbour, the small logging settlement that had grown up on the south shore of Burrard Inlet to process the massive trees covering what is now North Vancouver. Many people in the community worked at Hastings Mill and then gathered in "Gassy Jack" Deighton's hotel to drink and tell tall tales. When the decision was made to make Coal Harbour the western terminal of the Canadian Pacific Railway, the rough-and-ready settlement was transformed.

In 1885, the newly named townsite of Vancouver was laid out, and in 1886 Vancouver was incorporated. Two months later, a fire burned most of the city to the ground. Almost 800 buildings were destroyed and 13 people were killed. Rebuilding began immediately, and when the first transcontinental train rolled into Vancouver's Burrard Inlet terminal in 1887, the city boasted 5000 inhabitants.

With the advantages of a railway and a good natural harbour,

Vancouver continued to grow. Cargo ships brought tea and silk from Asia, pleasure liners carried visitors, and the railway transported settlers and entrepreneurs from other parts of Canada. Streets were paved, schools were built and factories were started. By 1900, Vancouver had outgrown the capital city of Victoria and was on its way to becoming the busiest city in the province.

At the same time as Vancouver was developing into a major commercial and manufacturing centre, communities in other parts

The tiny community of Coal Harbour was renamed Vancouver and grew by leaps and bounds once it was chosen as the CPR's western terminal. Seen here: the arrival in 1887 of the first trans-continental train into the city *(right)*; the Old Hastings Mill Store, now a museum, is Vancouver's oldest building, one of the few that escaped the 1886 fire *(above left)*; a stroll in Stanley Park, which opened in 1888, quickly became a favourite way to spend a Sunday afternoon *(above right)*.

of British Columbia were expanding. Since mineral production was so important to the province's economy, many of these communities were mining towns. On Vancouver Island, Nanaimo grew to serve workers who mined coal in damp, dark and often dangerous conditions. On the mainland, rich deposits of copper, silver and lead were discovered in the Kootenay region and hastened the establishment of Nelson as a supply centre. While neither Nanaimo nor Nelson rivalled Vancouver in size, they represented the kind of growth that was opening up more parts of the province.

Railway Expansion

From the 1880s to the early 1900s, the Canadian Pacific Railway played as large a role in British Columbia's development as the Hudson's Bay Company had played 50 years earlier. After completing its cross-Canada route in 1885, the CPR purchased hotels and ships, moved into mining and expanded its rail lines.

New routes built by the CPR and rival railway companies began to criss-cross British Columbia. The Canadian Northern Railway built a line that used the Yellowhead Pass through the Rockies and proceeded along the North Thompson River to Kamloops before running parallel with the CPR line through the Fraser Canyon to the coast. The Grand Trunk Pacific Railway began work in 1906 on a line that crossed from the Yellowhead Pass to Prince George and then continued on to the coast at Prince Rupert. Communities grew up all along these railway routes, and speculators bought land in the hope of selling it later at a profit. As rail lines spread, more and more settlers arrived from across Canada and around the world.

Immigration

In the 30 years that followed the completion of the CPR, British Columbia's Native population decreased dramatically, and the non-Native population increased even more so. Most of this increase resulted from immigration. Chinese immigrants arrived to join relatives who had come earlier to mine for gold and build the railway. Doukhobors came to escape religious persecution in their homeland. English, Irish, Scottish, Scandinavian, Italian and German immigrants came looking for opportunities not available in their crowded home countries, as did immigrants from India and Japan.

The vast majority of new arrivals in the 1880s, however, came from other parts of Canada. Looking for good farmland and better wages, young men and women left Ontario and the Maritimes to work as loggers, schoolteachers, cooks and shopkeepers in British Columbia. Canadian immigrants continued to arrive throughout the 1890s, outnumbering all other groups of new arrivals until the early 1900s, when British immigrants became the largest group of new British Columbians.

Throughout this period of steady immigration, people from Britain, northern Europe, the United States and other parts of

Below: **Japanese shop damaged during the 1907 anti-Asian riots.** *Right:* **Would-be Sikh immigrants aboard the *Komagata Maru*. After two months in harbour, the ship was finally persuaded to leave by the arrival of a Canadian navy cruiser.**

Canada were considered more desirable than immigrants from southern Europe and Asia. As the province grew, so did racist attitudes and policies. Chinese and Japanese people were termed an "Oriental menace" while East Indians were all called "Hindoos," even though most were Sikhs. Asian workers were excluded from many occupations, and Chinese immigrants had to pay a large "head tax" before entering the country. In Vancouver in 1907, a protest meeting of working men opposed to Asian immigration was followed by rioting in Chinatown and the Japanese area nearby. Later, the federal government passed laws to limit the numbers of people from Asia allowed into Canada.

One of the laws used to restrict Asian immigration required immigrants to travel directly from their country of origin to Canada. This law was challenged in the summer of 1914 by a wealthy Sikh who tried to bring in 376 Sikh and Muslim Punjabi immigrants on the *Komagata Maru*, which had made stops at Shanghai and Japan on its way to Canada from Hong Kong. Officials upholding the "continuous passage" law refused to let the ship land. The immigrants were kept on board the crowded steamer for two months while the Sikh organizer of the trip argued with immigration officials. Finally the officials had their way and the *Komagata Maru* and her passengers left for Hong Kong.

Unrest and Reform

Tensions caused by racial differences were not the only ones felt by British Columbians in the years before the First World War. Conflicts between workers and their employers were common in both the mining and fishing industries. In the early 1900s, British Columbia had more strikes than any other province, as workers fought against long hours, poor pay and unsafe working conditions.

In 1909, a gas explosion at a Vancouver Island coal mine killed 32 men. An investigation suggested that the company was more interested in making money than in protecting workers. Miners responded by joining a mine worker's union. A few years later, the company's refusal to act on a workers' gas safety report led to a two-year strike. From 1912 to 1914, almost 7000 miners refused to work, and the company kept its mines in partial operation using nonunion labour. In the summer of 1913, the striking workers learned that the company planned to bring in even more nonunion labour and riots broke out. Over 250 miners were arrested, and some were sentenced to as long as two years in prison. The provincial and the federal governments were clearly on the side of the employers, and the next year strikers were forced to accept a settlement that did not include recognition of the union.

The unrest among miners was matched by the unrest among fishers and cannery workers. The cannery owners controlled both the price paid for fish and the wages offered to workers. Labour leaders tried to improve wages and working conditions, but little was achieved because Native, Japanese and white workers in the fishing industry were unable to unite against their employers.

Later in the twentieth century, workers in both the fishing and the mining industries achieved better pay, hours and working conditions, but they did not have great success in their early campaigns for labour reform. Similarly, the campaign for women's suffrage — the right to vote — did not make much progress in the first years of the twentieth century. But this changed after 1910, when more suffrage associations were founded, and reformers like Helen Gregory MacGill and Helena Gutteridge became active in the campaign to improve the position of women in British Columbia. MacGill worked to change the legal status of women and children, who had little control over their own lives, and later became the first woman judge appointed in the province. Gutteridge campaigned for the rights of working women, who were paid much less than men, and later was elected to Vancouver City Council.

Campaigns for workers' and women's rights in the early 1900s were part of a larger reform movement that sought economic and

Helen Gregory MacGill in 1938, just after she received an honorary Doctor of Laws degree from the University of British Columbia. This was the first honorary degree conferred on a woman by the provincial university.

social change. In British Columbia, as elsewhere, the pace of change quickened after the outbreak of the First World War.

The First World War

On August 4, 1914, Britain declared war on Germany, and Canada, as part of the British Empire, was automatically drawn into the conflict. For four years, Canadians stood beside soldiers from Britain, France, Russia and other countries against soldiers from Germany, Austria-Hungary and Turkey. Millions of Canadian men fought in the war's muddy trenches, and over 3000 women served as nurses — called "bluebirds" because of their blue uniforms.

The war changed many aspects of life in British Columbia: communities became smaller as men and women left for Europe, certain industries expanded to serve the war effort, and the building of roads, bridges and other public works stopped. British Columbia contributed a larger share of its population to the war than any other Canadian province. Men and women of all backgrounds volunteered to serve as soldiers, cooks, ambulance drivers and nurses. Japanese, Sikh and Native British Columbians were among the 43 000 men who went overseas. By the end of the war, 6225 were dead and over 13 000 were wounded. Cities and towns across the province lost many of their young men. In Walhachin, a fruit-growing centre near Kamloops Lake in the central interior, all 43 young men in the 150-member community volunteered.

While the war disrupted family and community life, it also forced employers to negotiate with workers, who were needed to keep important industries running, and hastened women's suffrage (women were given the right to vote in provincial elections in 1917). As well, the wartime need for wood, certain metals and fish maintained the British Columbia economy.

After the War

Immediately after the war, the demand for British Columbia's natural resources decreased and the number of unemployed increased. Soldiers came home from Europe to find a province in economic difficulty. Everywhere in the province, the logging industry suffered when wood was no longer needed to manufacture British airplanes. In the interior mines and smelters were closing, and on the coast the fishery was in trouble. Problems in the fishery had started before the war with the building of the Canadian Northern Railway. In 1913, landslides caused by construction had partially blocked the Fraser River at Hell's Gate. Native fishers had made a heroic effort to net individual salmon and carry them upriver past the slide debris, but too few salmon had survived to spawn. The "lost generation" of fish and the blocked river meant that the Fraser River sockeye run was reduced to a fraction of its original size in the postwar years.

To stimulate the economy and help returning soldiers, Liberal premier John Oliver encouraged settlement in undeveloped areas like the Bulkley Valley and the Kootenays. Oliver's predecessor, Richard McBride, had focused on railway building and the expanding resource industries during his largely prosperous

1903-1915 term as premier. Oliver, a Delta farmer, concentrated instead on road building and farming during his less prosperous 1918-1927 term. One of the farming schemes involved draining Sumas Lake in the Fraser Valley south of Chilliwack and starting dairy farms. Another scheme involved irrigating the southern end of the Okanagan Valley and establishing fruit-growing communities. Oliver also negotiated the return to the province of a rich square of farmland known as the Peace River Block, which had been transferred to the federal government in 1884 as part of the terms for the completion of the Canadian Pacific Railway.

From 1920 onwards, the province experienced increased economic growth. In Vancouver, shipping was becoming the city's biggest industry, and many new homes and larger buildings were constructed. Victoria was expanding as well, becoming a popular tourist destination and a desirable retirement community. Throughout the province labour unrest lessened as more British Columbians found employment and benefited from new workers' compensation and pension programs. To British Columbians driving along the province's new dirt roads in Model-T Ford cars and trucks, the "good life" seemed within reach.

Left: Irrigation in the southern Okanagan Valley was first undertaken in the 1920s. The result over the next few decades was to transform the area into the major fruit-producing region it is today. *Below:* Vancouver Harbour in the 1920s

CHAPTER 6
New Challenges

The mid- to late 1920s were good years for most British Columbians. Prairie grain was shipped out of Vancouver in ever-increasing amounts, and the province's wood, minerals and fish were in demand around the world. Jobs were easy to find, and wages had increased since the war.

Greater prosperity meant that more people were buying things that they had once made at home — clothing, furniture and numerous food products. Local merchants did well, as did manufacturers in central Canada, who produced almost all of the province's manufactured goods. The government continued to promote farming schemes — even though most parts of the province did not have the right kinds of soil or climate for agriculture — while mining, logging and fishing expanded.

The Great Depression

On Black Thursday, October 29, 1929, prosperity ended when the New York stock market collapsed and a worldwide depression began. Unlike previous "slumps," or recessions, this was a deep and far-reaching economic disaster. British Columbians who had become used to prosperity suddenly found themselves out of work in a world that could no longer afford the province's natural resources or products. Prairie grain shipments fell, first because of reduced demand and then because of a drought that turned rich farmlands into dusty wastelands. Across Canada, the United States and

Vancouver's stunning Canada Place was built as the Canadian pavilion for Expo 86. It now houses a trade centre, a convention centre, a 500-room luxury hotel and a cruise ship terminal.

Europe, factories closed and unemployed men and women lined up to receive some form of government relief.

All British Columbians suffered during the years now known as the Great Depression. People lost their homes when they could not pay their taxes, and families were separated when breadwinners travelled away to find work. Some British Columbians suffered more than others. Women were not considered to be part of the workforce in the same way that men were. When single unemployed women in Vancouver tried to get relief money, they were told to find jobs as domestic servants. When unemployed Chinese British Columbians were given relief money, they were given less than non-Chinese British Columbians.

The hardships of the Depression forced everyone to manage with very little. People borrowed, bartered and improvised. Some wore clothes made out of old flour sacks and lived on home-grown produce, game and bannock. Some made soap from bear oil and moose fat, and coffee from roasted grain. Many chopped firewood and built their own homes, returning to the pioneering traditions of earlier years.

People in rural British Columbia had some advantages over city-

Police armed with clubs and tear gas drive unemployed demonstrators out of Vancouver's main post office, July 20, 1938.

dwellers. In the country, people were used to providing for themselves and helping each other. In cities, hunting and fishing were not practical ways of putting food on the table.

Cities were also places where large numbers of unemployed men gathered. In Vancouver in 1938, there were 6000 jobless men, many from the drought-stricken Prairies. When the provincial government refused to give relief payments to non-British Columbians, 1000 unemployed men took over the main post office, the art gallery and the Georgia Hotel. Those occupying the art gallery and the hotel agreed to leave on their own, but the group occupying the post office had to be driven out by police using tear gas and clubs. Many people were wounded in the confrontation.

The Second World War

On September 3, 1939, Britain declared war on Germany after the German army invaded Poland. A week later, Canada declared war on Germany and became part of a conflict that eventually would involve many more countries and would rage for six years in Europe, Africa, Asia and the South Pacific. During the conflict, 42 042 Canadians lost their lives.

In British Columbia, the declaration of war led to an immediate drop in the number of unemployed when many men enlisted in the army, navy or air force. Later, women became directly involved in the war effort as well. By the end of the Second World War, over 4000 nurses had served in more than 100 hospital units, and many more women had served in the Royal Canadian Air Force, Canadian Women's Army Corps and Royal Canadian Naval Women's Service.

Men and women served on the home front as well as the battle front throughout the war. Shipbuilding became an important industry, employing over 30 000 workers in Victoria and Greater Vancouver. The logging industry also employed large numbers of people. Sitka spruce from the Queen Charlotte Islands was needed to build the light frames of Mosquito bombers, and fir was needed for war-time housing. The mining industry benefited from war-time demands for metals and fuels, but also from the opening up of British Columbia's north.

The Alaska Highway — stretching 2445 kilometres (1519 miles) from Dawson Creek in the Peace River country to Fairbanks, Alaska — was completed as an American defence project in 1943. As well as providing the U.S. army with access to territory that was vulnerable to Japanese attack, the highway provided access for mineral exploration. Old fur-trade posts like Fort St. John and Fort Nelson developed into modern communities to serve prospectors and mine employees as well as people travelling the Alaska Highway.

Although many British Columbians prospered from war-time growth and change, some did not. After Japan bombed Pearl Harbour in 1941, British Columbians of Japanese descent were treated as potential allies of a country many had never seen, much less supported. At first, only a few Japanese men, along with German and Italian "enemy aliens," were evacuated from coastal areas. Then, as fear of a Japanese invasion increased, full-scale evacuation and internment began. Thousands of Japanese men, women and children — most of them Canadian citizens — were rounded up and sent to inland communities and work camps. Many were given little time to gather their possessions, and many had to watch as government officials took away their property. The loss of homes, fishing boats and businesses made it very difficult for evacuees to re-establish themselves after the war. There was some improvement in 1949 when people of Japanese ancestry were allowed to live on the West Coast again and were given the right to vote in federal and provincial elections. However, it was not until 1988 that the Canadian government officially apologized to Japanese British Columbians and attempted to compensate them for losses during the war.

Left: A famous photograph of a Vancouver family's leave-taking early in the Second World War. *Above:* In British Columbia, as in the rest of Canada, the war years saw many women take on jobs traditionally done by men.

"The Golden Age"

After the Second World War, British Columbia entered a new era of growth and prosperity. Demand for the province's natural resources did not end with the close of the war, and once again forestry, mining, agriculture and fishing were able to provide jobs and products for many people. Tourism and manufacturing also began to play larger roles in the provincial economy.

From 1947 onwards, a wave of Dutch, German, Italian, Greek and Portuguese immigrants joined the flow of British immigrants arriving in the province. Many "war brides" from England and Europe arrived to join their Canadian soldier husbands. In 1951 the population of British Columbia was 1 165 210.

In 1952, dissatisfaction with the previous Conservative, Liberal and coalition governments led to the election of the province's first Social Credit government. Socred Premier W.A.C. ("Wacky")

Bennett, a Kelowna hardware merchant, was a charismatic man of the people who kept the party in power for the next 20 years. Early on, the Social Credit government undertook a range of major projects designed to "open up" British Columbia. From 1955 to 1968, the energetic minister of highways, P.A. "Flying Phil" Gagliardi, pushed roads into every corner of the province, making areas in the northeast and northwest accessible for industry and tourism. In 1958 alone, 62 bridges and six ferry landings were built. In 1962, the final B.C. portion of the Trans-Canada Highway was completed.

As roads were built to link remote parts of the province and air travel became more common, water transport changed. The Union Steamship Company had been running boats between tiny coastal communities for 70 years when it stopped operating in 1959. A year later the provincial government began operating ferries to Vancouver Island. Soon a fleet of blue-and-white vessels was transporting commuters and visitors.

Big hydroelectric projects were also popular during the years Bennett was in power. In the 1950s, Alcan built an aluminum smelter at the head of Kitimat Arm on the north coast and dammed the Nechako River south of Fraser Lake to provide power. The entirely new community of Kitimat was built for the many families that moved into the area. In 1968, the Peace River development in the northeast began providing low-cost electricity to major companies investing in the province.

The Aluminum Company of Canada built a giant smelter in the northern B.C. wilderness in the early 1950s, then built the town of Kitimat around it. The facility remains the only aluminum smelter in Canada outside Quebec.

Prosperity and a greater sense of confidence during the postwar years led to a greater interest in the arts and education. The Queen Elizabeth Theatre and the Vancouver Playhouse were built, and an opera company was formed. Museums, galleries, schools and colleges opened. In Hazelton, Native and non-Native people worked together to build a carving school, workshop and museum in a recreated 1880s Gitksan village called 'Ksan. Victoria College in the capital became the University of Victoria in 1963, and in Burnaby, Simon Fraser University welcomed its first students in 1965. British Columbians in most parts of the province benefited from a buoyant North American economy.

Towards the Twenty-First Century

As W.A.C. Bennett's 20 years in power came to an end, unemployment and labour unrest once again began to affect British Columbians. Hopes for continued prosperity were disappointed as inflation increased and businesses failed. In 1972, the New Democratic Party (NDP) came into power in the province for the first time. Under Premier Dave Barrett, a former social worker from working-class East Vancouver, the NDP government tried to make changes it considered long overdue. During its first year in power, the new government rushed 400 bills through the legislature. Among other things, the bills reorganized social services and created new labour laws. But with the world economy entering a severe recession, the Barrett government's push for change and continued spending made many voters unhappy.

In 1975, the Social Credit Party was returned to power under W.A.C. Bennett's son, Bill Bennett. Subsequently, another "Bill," Wilhelmus Vander Zalm, became leader of the Social Credit Party and premier of British Columbia. A colourful and controversial premier, Vander Zalm was eventually rejected by many Social Credit supporters. His successor, Rita Johnston, became the province's first woman premier, but her time in office was brief.

Since being taken over by the government in 1960, B.C.'s ferry system has grown and modernized. Today, it is one of the largest and most sophisticated in the world.

The 1991 election, held shortly after Johnston became party leader and premier, resulted in an NDP government. The newly elected premier, Mike Harcourt, soon faced many challenges — some that would have been familiar to his predecessors, some that were new.

Issues Old and New

Today, British Columbia is still the vast and rugged province it was at the time of Confederation. But instead of an 1871 population of 36 000, it now has a population of 3.2 million. Rather than living on homesteads and in small mining or logging communities, most British Columbians now live in the expanding cities of the province's southwest.

Economic uncertainty continues to plague British Columbia. The fishing industry is suffering because of shrinking fish populations. Mining, as in the past, is suffering from fluctuations in demand for particular minerals. And the forest industry is suffering because of dwindling supplies of trees — years of overcutting now mean that tough decisions must be made about how many trees can be cut in the future.

The forest industry is also being forced to decide where trees can be cut. Individuals and environmental groups are opposed to logging in certain areas of the province. As well, some British Columbians are opposed to clear-cut logging, and a number of

The Museum of Anthropology at the University of British Columbia, built in the 1970s, houses one of the world's finest collections of Northwest Coast Native art and artifacts.

Native groups want any kind of logging stopped on lands they claim as their own.

Today, a variety of Native organizations in the province are working to reclaim traditional territories. Many First Nations groups are also moving towards self-government. One on the Sunshine Coast in southern British Columbia negotiated a self-government agreement with federal and provincial officials: since 1988, the Sechelt Nation has been in control of its reserve lands and has operated along the lines of a municipality. Its success has made many other British Columbians and Canadians recognize the need to permit self-government and settle Native land claims.

Even with the positive changes in attitude towards Native peoples, racism is still very much an issue in British Columbia. Chinese immigrants no longer pay "head tax" and citizens of Japanese descent do not live in internment camps, but there is still an uneasy blending of races and cultures in the province. As immigrants and refugees continue to arrive from all parts of the world — Asia, Eastern Europe, Central America, Africa — the face of British Columbia is changing. Along with economic and environmental challenges, British Columbia's leaders face various social challenges. Over the next decade, they will be working to make citizens of both sexes, all income levels and every colour, culture and background feel included in provincial decision making.

CHAPTER 7
Government

Like all the provinces, British Columbia has a government based on the British parliamentary model. At the head is the lieutenant-governor, the Queen's representative, who is appointed for a five-year term by the governor general of Canada on the advice of the prime minister. The province is divided into 75 legislative constituencies. The people of each constituency or riding elect a representative to be their MLA (Member of the Legislative Assembly). Elections cannot be more than five years apart.

Following an election, the lieutenant-governor calls on the leader of the political party with the largest number of elected members to serve as premier. The premier then chooses a cabinet from the elected members of the party. Members of the cabinet head government ministries such as forestry, finance and tourism. The premier and cabinet form the executive council, which runs the government, while the legislature enacts laws. These laws concern all aspects of life in British Columbia: economic development, social services, road building and, of course, taxes.

Before a law is approved by the legislature, it is proposed as a bill, which must pass through a long review process. Part of this process includes consideration by a committee made up of members of all political parties. At that time, members of the public, businesses and concerned groups can present their viewpoints. In recent years, this process has been used to try to resolve disagreements among the forest industry, environmentalists and other interest groups. This process means that the citizens of

The British Columbia Legislative Building, Victoria. Rising above the central dome is a statue of Captain George Vancouver.

British Columbia can be involved in their province's decision making before a bill becomes law.

Through the first half of the 1900s, Liberals and Conservatives dominated British Columbia politics. In 1952, the Social Credit Party was established by former Conservatives led by W.A.C. Bennett. Since then, the Social Credit Party and the New Democratic Party (NDP) have controlled the province's political life. Generally, Social Credit favours free enterprise, while the NDP represents government involvement in economic and social concerns.

The provincial government administers a wide range of programs for British Columbia. Taxes are used to provide social services and to encourage development of the provincial economy. Provincial social services include major programs for health, education, child protection, income assistance and housing. Other provincial programs safeguard human rights, provide law enforcement and protect the environment. The province shares the cost of some programs, such as the public school system, with municipalities. As well, the federal government shares the costs for some services.

Other Levels of Government

British Columbia is represented by 32 members of Parliament in the House of Commons. Canada's first female prime minister, Kim Campbell, came from British Columbia. There are also six appointed representatives in the Senate.

The province has 41 cities, 51 district municipalities, 14 towns, 44 villages and 29 regional districts. These cover 80 percent of the population but only one percent of British Columbia's total area! The other 99 percent of the province is classified as "Unorganized Territory" with no specific local government.

The Court System

The judicial system has come a long way in British Columbia since Judge Matthew Baillie Begbie rode his horse to makeshift courts set

Contrasting courthouses: Kamloops (*left*) and the new Vancouver Law Courts, designed by Arthur Erickson

up in the bush around the province. Today, three levels of courts maintain the law in the province.

The Provincial Court is the first level in British Columbia's court system, and it is here that most cases are heard. There is no jury in this court. The provincial government appoints the judges. These 125 judges deal with minor criminal offences, such as shoplifting, family and youth problems, traffic violations and money claims under $10 000.

The next level in the court system is the Supreme Court. Here most cases are heard by judge and jury, or sometimes by judge alone. The federal government appoints judges to this court, which hears many civil cases, including divorce, libel and financial disputes greater than $10 000. It also hears serious criminal cases that include murder and manslaughter, aggravated assault, bank robbery and major drug crimes. As well, the Supreme Court hears some appeals from Provincial Court.

The Court of Appeal is the highest court in the province. It is not a trial court. Three to five judges sit together on a panel and hear appeals from the two other courts concerning criminal and civil cases. The chief justice of British Columbia heads the Court of Appeal. An appeal case involves only the judges and lawyers. Court of Appeal judges are appointed by the federal government.

Education

British Columbia has 75 local school districts in its public education system. Under the School Act, each district is governed by an elected board of trustees. In 1992, there were 1599 public schools. Approximately 527 000 students attended 1155 elementary schools and 444 secondary and combination schools.

Public education is non-denominational and paid for through provincial taxes. The province also has 246 independent schools with 37 000 students. Families must pay a fee or tuition for their children to attend these schools.

While the majority of students attend public or independent

Above : Simon Fraser University was built in the 1960s on top of Burnaby Mountain just outside Vancouver. *Right:* Students and teacher gather around a computer at a Sikh school in suburban Vancouver. *Far right:* The First Nations House of Learning at the University of British Columbia opened in 1993.

schools, some students study at home. Pioneers in British Columbia were often so isolated that no schools were available to them. As a solution, provincial correspondence education was introduced, first in 1919 at the elementary level, and ten years later at the secondary level. It is still used by British Columbians living in remote areas.

A wide range of academic, technical, vocational and career education programs is offered at 15 community colleges throughout the province, and at the British Columbia Institute of Technology and the Emily Carr College of Art and Design.

British Columbia has four publicly funded universities, which offer a host of courses in undergraduate, graduate and professional programs. The University of British Columbia is in Vancouver; Simon Fraser University is in Burnaby; the University of Victoria is in Victoria; and the main campus of the new University of Northern British Columbia is in Prince George. Some community colleges also offer university programs in partnership with the universities.

Because of its many remote communities, the province has placed a high priority on distance education. The Open University offers degree programs in the arts, while the Open College offers programs in such fields as health, business and tourism. The Knowledge Network provides general public education for adults and children on television.

Health

The Hospital Insurance Act ensures that all permanent residents of British Columbia have access to medical care. One group that receives special attention is the elderly. The province's pleasant, mild climate is very attractive to senior citizens, and as a result, a larger proportion of retired people live in British Columbia than in other provinces. One-quarter of the population of Victoria is over 65. Government-sponsored long-term care programs ensure good quality care for the elderly.

CHAPTER 8
The Economy

Over the centuries, different products have been important to the economy of British Columbia. Five hundred years ago, the Native peoples of the region made and traded a variety of goods: dried berries, jewellery, cedar boxes, blankets made of mountain goat wool, and many other items. Later, European settlers arrived in large numbers and began to make and exchange goods: furs, gold, salmon and lumber for shipbuilding. Today British Columbians offer numerous services and make and sell many products, from gourmet foods to award-winning films.

Natural resources form the backbone of British Columbia's economy. Wood, metals, hydroelectricity and fish have all played their part in the past and continue to do so. Four important sectors of today's provincial economy are forestry, mining, energy and fishing. These industries earn approximately 80 percent of the money made from exporting goods.

Most of the goods exported go to the United States, Japan and South Korea. Although the United States is British Columbia's chief trading partner, countries in the Asia-Pacific region buy 40 percent of its exports. Trade experts think that these countries will play an even larger role in the province's economy in the future.

Forestry

Forests and the forest industry are very important to British Columbians. Thousands of people work at jobs in the forest industry, and more than half of the province's exports are forest

The Hugh Keenleyside dam on the Columbia River was built in the late 1960s as part of a huge hydroelectric development project.

products. Most of the trees harvested are softwoods — spruce, lodgepole pine, true fir (or balsam), hemlock, cedar and Douglas fir — and are used to make lumber, pulp and paper products, shingles and shakes. Some of the people involved are loggers, biologists, truck drivers, paper mill workers and tree planters.

Whether they are employed making forest products or not, all British Columbians have a stake in the forest industry. Eighty-five percent of the province's area is designated as Provincial Forests and is owned by the people of the province. This land is managed by the government through the B.C. Forest Service (BCFS), which grants Forest Licences and Tree Farm Licences to forest companies. These licences give the companies cutting rights and responsibilities. The companies' responsibilities include road building and tree planting (or reforestation) in the logged areas.

Before the Second World War, the methods and equipment used to harvest and process wood required many workers. Logging operations and small mills were found in and near the forests all over the province. After the war, logging changed. Forest products began to be processed in large, centrally located plants. Fewer people were needed to harvest and process the wood.

Right: "Fallers" in a stand of Douglas fir on Vancouver Island. *Far right:* Vancouver sawmill. B.C. produces about two-thirds of Canada's sawn lumber.

Today, as more efficient logging equipment has become available, trees are cut at a faster rate and supplies of easy-to-reach trees have grown smaller. Even with reforestation programs, not enough trees have grown to replace the ones logged.

The dwindling supply of trees is not the only problem the forest industry faces. Today there is a great deal of conflict between forest companies and other groups in the province. Some British Columbians are unhappy about certain land-use decisions. There have been disputes over whether logging should be allowed in some places, including the Queen Charlotte Islands, the Cariboo Mountains area, the Walbran Valley and Clayoquot Sound. There have also been disputes about logging methods. Many people oppose clearcutting — the removal of large areas of forest at one time — which they say damages the environment.

Everyone in British Columbia wants something when it comes to forests and forestry. First Nations governments want their land claims settled. Forest workers want to protect their jobs and communities. Resort operators want to prohibit unsightly clearcuts

Clearcut area in Vancouver Island's Carmanah Valley. In recent years logging practices — particularly the logging of old-growth forests and clearcutting — have stirred up a great deal of opposition from environmentalists and other groups.

in places tourists visit. Pulp and paper mill owners want a reliable supply of wood for the future. Environmental groups want to preserve the old-growth forests and watersheds that support animal life and contain trees that are hundreds of years old.

In an attempt to resolve forest industry disputes, the government established the Commission on Resources and the Environment (CORE) in 1992. CORE is now working with concerned groups to find a way to protect both the forest industry and the environment.

Mining

Most of British Columbia lies within the Western Cordillera, a geological formation that contains a wide variety of valuable minerals. Minerals found in the province include gold, coal, asbestos, sulphur, copper, silver, zinc, lead and molybdenum.

The miners, prospectors, engineers, heavy equipment operators, clerical workers and others employed in the mining industry might live in one of many areas. In the far north, the mine at Cassiar produces asbestos. On the north coast, the smelter at Kitimat processes aluminum. Sulphur is produced in Peace River country; coal is mined in the southeast corner of the province. And in the southern Okanagan, silver, lead and zinc are extracted.

In 1991, the value of mineral production in British Columbia was $3.6 billion. Copper accounted for $834 million of this amount, gold for another $244 million and silver for $78 million. Lead, zinc, molybdenum and coal were also important in 1991.

Mining suffers more than most industries from changes in the market for its products. The need for particular minerals can swing dramatically, carrying a town from "boom" to "bust" in a very short time. This has happened often in the province, particularly in communities where the mine is the main employer.

Besides having to deal with unpredictable markets, the mining industry also has to deal with some public opposition. British Columbians have become concerned about the damage mineral

Clockwise from top:
**Open pit coal mine
in the Elk River
Valley; lead-zinc
mine and the
Cominco smelter at
Trail where its ore is
processed**

extraction can do to an area's plant life, soil and water. In 1993, the
government responded to public concerns and declared that there
would be no mining in the Tatshenshini River Valley in the far
northwest, even though vast copper deposits are present there. In
the future, CORE will be considering other cases where mining
may be in conflict with the preservation of an environmentally
sensitive area.

Energy

British Columbia is rich in energy resources. Oil and natural gas are
found in the northeast, and coal is found in the north, southwest
and southeast. Waterways that can be used to generate electricity
are found almost everywhere in the province. Only petroleum,
which comes mainly from Alberta, must be imported.

There are five coal producers in the East Kootenay-Crowsnest coalfields, two in the northeast coalfields and one on Vancouver Island. These producers send most of their coal to Roberts Bank, near Vancouver, where it is loaded on bulk-carriers and sent to Pacific Rim countries.

Meanwhile, in the northeastern part of the province, oil and gas are piped down the Westcoast Energy Pipeline from the Peace River district to Vancouver and Washington state. Other pipelines serve the Cariboo, Okanagan and Kootenay districts. The Vancouver Island pipeline, completed in 1991, provides gas to the Sunshine Coast and Vancouver Island.

From various parts of British Columbia, transmission lines carry electricity made by harnessing the power of the province's great rivers: the Peace, the Fraser, the Skeena and the Columbia. Eighteen percent of British Columbia's requirement is provided by hydroelectric dams. One of the largest of these is the W.A.C. Bennett Dam on the Peace River. During the excavation for the dam, workers found a trail of dinosaur footprints in the mud. These footprints were thought to be at least 100 million years old.

Although British Columbia has abundant energy resources, the production, transportation and use of these resources is not problem-

Right: On the Sechelt Peninsula, workers get ready to join sections of pipe on the Vancouver Island gas pipeline. *Far right:* "Nodding donkey" at sunrise in the northeastern corner of the province, where B.C.'s only oil fields are found

free. The public today is concerned about environmental damage caused by coal mining, dam building and pipeline construction. The air pollution caused by burning fossil fuels worries many people as well. Cleaner fuels, alternative energy sources and more efficient resource use will all need to be part of the energy industry in the future.

Fishing

Fishing has supported people in British Columbia for thousands of years. Many Native groups obtained food and materials for tools and artwork from the sea and the rivers of the area. European settlers have relied on ocean resources as well.

Today the fishing and aquaculture industry in British Columbia harvests more than 40 species of fish and marine animals. There are over 240 fish-processing plants along the coast, numerous fish farms raising salmon or shellfish and at least 6200 vessels in the fishing fleet. Fishing here is big business.

Some of the people employed in the industry are fishboat operators, marine biologists, processing-plant workers and fish farmers. Prince Rupert in the north and Steveston in the south are important fishing centres where many of these people work.

Left: Worker at the Kootenay Trout Hatchery, Bull River. *Below:* Wharf with nets and fishing boats at Port Edward, at the mouth of the Skeena River

The several species of salmon found in B.C. waters are the focus of a lot of industry attention. Most fish farms raise salmon, and many commercial fishers make their livelihood catching pinks, sockeye, coho, chum and chinook. B.C. salmon — whether fresh, frozen or canned — is prized around the world and makes up more than half of the province's ocean exports. Herring, different kinds of groundfish and shellfish make up the rest.

In 1991, exports of fish and seafood products were valued at $635 million. Japan was the main customer, followed by the United States and the European Community. In Japan, the mass of eggs or roe found in herring is a traditional delicacy. Each spring the B.C. herring fishery gears up to satisfy this export market. Tonnes of herring are caught, the roe is taken out of the mature female fish, and the carcasses are processed for animal feed and fertilizer. Millions of dollars are made from the herring roe fishery.

Fishing, like forestry and mining, is not without opponents and difficulties. Many people are concerned about shrinking fish populations. Several groups have been accused of overfishing: commercial fishers, sport fishers and Native fishers. Fisheries biologists are working to assess the situation. Whoever and whatever is to blame for the decline in fish stocks, changes will undoubtedly be made in fishing practices and regulations over the next few years.

Manufacturing

British Columbia's manufacturing industry is based mainly on natural resources. The processing of logs, the refining of petroleum or minerals and the production of food employ many British Columbians. In 1991, manufacturing shipments were valued at $23 billion. These shipments included wood and paper products as well as a range of food products: fruit drinks and wine, processed fish, poultry and various products made from milk, eggs, beef or pork.

Some of the secondary manufacturing industries involve metal and chemical products, printing and publishing, electronics and clothing.

Manufacturing activity is centred in the Vancouver area and on the east coast of Vancouver Island. Efforts are being made to develop other manufacturing centres and to expand the manufacturing sector by "adding more value" to natural resources. Furniture and plastics are examples of value-added products that British Columbians hope to see more of in the future.

Tourism

Tourism is a major dollar earner in British Columbia. In 1991, revenue from overnight visitors reached over $5 billion, and the industry employs large numbers of British Columbians all over the province.

On the southern coast, the mild climates of Vancouver and Victoria attract visitors year-round. In the past, Expo 86 and the Clinton-Yeltsin 1993 Leaders' Summit brought many visitors and focused world attention on the province. Other events, like the World Cup Ski Races at Whistler and the annual Indy 500 Car Races, draw sports fans on a regular basis.

On the east and west coasts of Vancouver Island and on the northern coast of the mainland, visitors from around the world catch salmon, trout and steelhead. River rafting, canoeing, kayaking and

Magnificent scenery and a wide range of recreational activities are just two of the attractions that draw millions of tourists to British Columbia.

surfing are other activities that draw visitors to these areas. Away from the coast, numerous resorts attract downhill and cross-country skiers in the winter, and golfers, tennis players, hikers and cyclists in the summer. Other visitors are interested in the province's history, and probably more are interested in the wide variety of wildlife to be seen.

Whatever their interests, most of the province's visitors come from other parts of Canada and the United States. Overseas visitors come principally from Japan, then from the United Kingdom and Germany. To improve service for these visitors, the provincial government has designed a training program called SuperHost, which teaches front-line workers in the industry how to give pleasant and efficient assistance to tourists. The program has been so successful that other provinces, American states and many countries have developed programs based on SuperHost.

Agriculture

Only 4 percent of the land in British Columbia is considered farmland, yet agriculture is the province's third-largest industry, ranking behind forestry and tourism. A third of the farmland is used to raise crops; the rest is used for pasture or grazing.

Throughout the province, British Columbians are busy operating dairy farms, market gardens, herb farms, cattle ranches, and pig and poultry farms. Farmers are at work in the vast wheat fields of the Peace River country and the small, intensively planted ginseng plots of the dry Nicola Valley. (Ginseng roots are highly prized in Asian medicine.) In the south and central interior, ranchers tend cattle on rolling rangeland. In the Okanagan Valley, fruit farmers grow apples, cherries, peaches, apricots and plums as well as grapes for the thriving wine industry. And in the mild climate of the Fraser Valley outside Vancouver, farmers grow vegetables, berries, mushrooms, bulbs and ornamental flowers. In 1991, the province's 19 225 farms earned over $1 billion.

Far left: **Farm in the Chilliwack area.**
Left: **Irrigated vineyards along the Similkameen River contrast sharply with the arid terrain beyond.**

Film Industry

British Columbia's fastest growing and most glamorous industry is the movie business. In 1991, 101 films and television shows were shot here, and, in 1992, production companies spent $211 million in the province.

While everyone agrees that the province's scenery is the real star of the industry, producers from all over the world like the variety of locations and appreciate the highly skilled workforce. British Columbia can provide actors, camera operators, makeup artists, special effects co-ordinators, location scouts and the many other specialists needed to work on film or TV productions.

TV series set here over the years include *The Beachcombers, Neon Rider* and *Northwood.* Notable among movies made in the province are B.C. filmmaker Sandy Wilson's *My American Cousin* and, more recently, *Impolite,* which impressed critics with its glowing portrayal of Vancouver.

Transportation

People and goods are transported in British Columbia by water, by rail, by road and by air. Vancouver is the province's main port and the second largest port in North America. In 1990, it handled over $38 billion in goods. Ships from Korea, Poland, South Africa, Japan and the Philippines can be seen in the deep waters of Burrard Inlet

Above: Coast guard and float plane dock, Prince Rupert. Planes like these provide important service to the province's remote communities. *Right:* The *Royal Hudson*, North America's only steam locomotive in scheduled mainline service

on any day of the year. Other year-round deep-sea ports are located at Prince Rupert, New Westminster, Victoria, Esquimault, Nanaimo, Port Alberni, Campbell River and Powell River. B.C. ports accommodate a range of cargo ships, freighters, research vessels, fishing boats and naval ships. Many also accommodate vessels belonging to the British Columbia Ferry Corporation. BC Ferries operates one of the largest ferry systems in the world. It has 27 routes between the Lower Mainland, Vancouver Island and various coastal ports. In 1990-91, it carried almost 20 million passengers and over seven million vehicles. The corporation's new *Spirit of B.C.*, a superferry launched in 1993, is one of the most sophisticated in the world.

British Columbia's railway system is less sophisticated but no less important. Over the years, 6800 kilometres (4225 miles) of railway track have been laid across the province. CN Rail and CP Rail operate freight lines, and VIA Rail operates a passenger line between Victoria and Courtenay. BC Rail operates both freight and passenger lines.

Every day in the summer, BC Rail's *Royal Hudson* chuffs from

North Vancouver to Squamish, sending up great plumes of steam as it skirts the sparking blue waters of Howe Sound. In summer and winter, BC Rail passenger cars shuttle between North Vancouver and Prince George, a trip that is rated one of the "top ten" scenic excursions in the world.

Although less scenic, air travel is also important in British Columbia. Vancouver International Airport is the province's largest airport, handling ten million passengers, on average, a year.

As far as roads go, British Columbia might still be considered a pioneer province. The highway network includes more unpaved roads (21 388 kilometres/ 13 290 miles) than paved ones (20 554 kilometres/12 772 miles). The mountainous terrain and the size of the province are both a challenge to road builders.

Communications

British Columbia's communications network links remote areas and numerous communities with each other and with locations around the world. People rely on telephones, facsimile machines, radios, televisions and newspapers to "keep in touch."

Over 98 percent of B.C. homes and businesses have telephone service. Even remote areas of the province have service, although this often takes the form of radio phones.

There are 87 radio stations. Over 82 percent of British Columbians subscribe to cable television services, and many people in remote areas pull in television signals with the help of a satellite dish. There are ten television stations that broadcast original programs, 259 rebroadcasting stations and 137 cable systems. Both television channels and radio stations offer multicultural programs.

Two newspapers, *The Sun* and the *Province*, are produced daily in Vancouver and shipped all around the province. Presses in other communities turn out 15 daily newspapers and over 160 weekly or community papers. Magazine and book publishers also keep British Columbians informed.

CHAPTER 9

Arts and Recreation

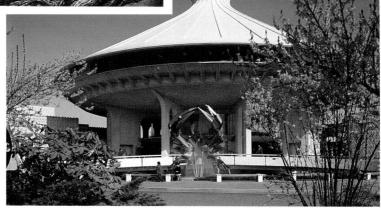

For centuries, the people of British Columbia have enjoyed a wealth of cultural traditions. Long ago, the Native peoples along the coast told legends that were passed on from one generation to the next. Dancers wearing elaborately carved masks often acted out these legends. Nootka and Kwakiutl shamans used the glimmering firelight in the longhouses and magic quartz crystals to create dramatic effects in their theatrical performances. Coastal peoples also carved totem poles and made bentwood boxes from a single piece of wood and decorated them with carvings and paintings. In the interior, Native peoples also told legends and sang songs, which were sometimes accompanied by drums, rattles and flutes.

Early immigrants from Europe brought their culture with them. During the gold rush, stock theatre companies performed English comedies and dramas. Sometimes they even staged scenes from Shakespeare's plays. The works of early painters and writers were European in style and technique. Gradually, however, artists began to paint and write about what they saw in British Columbia and to experiment with new styles.

Today the arts and recreation in British Columbia reflect the diversity of its population. You can admire Native totem poles and masks, enjoy Shakespeare on the beach, listen to music by Doukhobor choirs and watch Sikh wrestling.

Clockwise from top: **Bryan Adams in concert; Native mask, inlaid with mother-of-pearl, on display at the Museum of Anthropology, University of British Columbia; The H.R. MacMillan Planetarium, Vancouver;** *Logs: Ladysmith Harbour,* **by Vancouver Island landscape painter Edward John Hughes**

The Performing Arts

People in British Columbia who enjoy theatre, music, opera and dance have much to choose from. The province has more than 50 professional performing arts groups, ranging from traditional orchestras and theatre companies to experimental dance troupes and a horse-drawn stage company.

Theatre

Professional theatres began to emerge in British Columbia in the 1960s. The Vancouver Playhouse opened in 1963 and four years later created a sensation when it presented George Ryga's *The Ecstasy of Rita Joe*, the story of a young Native woman who suffers at the hands of white society. The following season, the Playhouse presented another play by George Ryga, *Grass and Wild Strawberries*, which included live rock music and invited members of the audience to come on stage to dance at the end of each performance. This play broke all previous box office records. Today you can see both classic and modern plays, including Canadian premieres and Broadway plays, at the Playhouse.

Vancouver is also the home of the Arts Club Theatre, the largest regional theatre in Western Canada. Located on bustling Granville Island, it offers drama, comedy and musicals, with an emphasis on twentieth-century productions. For those who prefer more experimental works, Tamahnous Theatre specializes in avant-garde theatre and has presented many plays based on dreams or fantasies. (The name "Tamahnous" comes from the Chilcotin word for "magic.") Touchstone Theatre and the Headlines Theatre Company often present plays that deal with social issues. Many other groups put on experimental plays at the Vancouver East Cultural Centre, a beautifully restored old church.

In summer, the Bard on the Beach Theatre Society presents Shakespearean favourites in an open-ended candy-striped tent in Vanier Park, affording a magnificent view of the city, the sea and the

Far left: With Vancouver as a backdrop, Torquil Campbell plays Romeo in the Bard on the Beach production of *Romeo and Juliet. Left:* British Columbia's reputation as a film and television production centre continues to grow. Seen here is the cast of the CBC's popular teen drama series, *Northwood.*

mountains. Summer is also the season for Broadway-style musicals staged at Stanley Park's Malkin Bowl Theatre under the Stars.

The first professional theatre in Victoria was the Bastion Theatre, founded in 1971. The Bastion, the McPherson and the Royal theatres all present dramas, comedies and musicals.

Throughout the province, hundreds of theatre groups entertain British Columbians. Every summer the Gold Rush Theatre in Barkerville puts on old-fashioned shows like those from the gold rush days. Also in the summer, the Caravan Stage Company travels by horse-drawn wagons to perform in small communities in the interior. In the little town of Horsefly, the whole community participates in the annual Follies. And on the Sunshine Coast, theatre buffs can hop into a four-wheel-drive "taxi" and go up a mountain to see a play staged in a Scout hall.

Besides George Ryga, well-known B.C. playwrights include John Gray and Carol Bolt. John Gray has written several musicals, and Carol Bolt writes plays about the problems of urban living. She also helped create the children's TV show *Fraggle Rock.* British Columbians who have gained fame on stage, screen and/or TV include Chief Dan George, Bruno Gerussi and Michael J. Fox.

Music

Music holds a prominent place in the cultural life of Vancouver. The Vancouver Symphony Orchestra and the Vancouver Bach Choir perform at the legendary Orpheum Theatre, where 100 glittering chandeliers light the halls. For something a little different, there is the ten-day International Jazz Festival in June, and every July, the Folk Music Festival held at Jericho Beach attracts thousands of folk music enthusiasts. Rock music fans can hear their favourite groups at B.C. Place Stadium or the Pacific Coliseum on the grounds of the Pacific National Exhibition.

At the Royal Theatre in Victoria, the Victoria Symphony performs pops, classics concerts and the Masterworks Series, which features music and artists from all over the world. Members of the symphony also put on special performances for schools. The Greater Victoria Youth Orchestra, composed of 60 musicians between the ages of 11 and 25, performs three or four programs of symphonic music a year.

In summer, music sounds throughout the province. Old-time piano music at the Theatre Royale in Barkerville echoes the sounds of the

Right: In keeping with its image as the "Bavarian City of the Canadian Rockies," Kimberley hosts the International Accordion Championships every summer. *Below right:* Every year on August 1, the Victoria Symphony holds its Symphony Splash, a free, open-air concert performed on a harbour barge to enthusiastic audiences that number in the tens of thousands.

gold rush days. In early June, Doukhobor choirs come to Castlegar from all over Canada to celebrate their music and traditions. The International Accordion Championship is held in Kimberley in July, and that same month Burns Lake hosts the Bluegrass Music Festival.

And, every summer, a grand piano is swung by helicopter to the top of Whistler Mountain, where Vancouver Symphony musicians provide an afternoon of classical music in the alpine meadows.

Notable among B.C. musicians who have achieved national and international recognition are classical composer Jean Coulthard, mezzo-soprano Judith Forst, children's entertainer Charlotte Diamond, country singer Patricia Conroy and rock superstar Bryan Adams, who grew up in North Vancouver. In the 1980s, Adams's albums *Reckless* and *Into the Fire* soared to the top of the charts. Tom Cochrane is another rock musician who lives in Vancouver.

Opera

Opera has always been strong in Victoria. The Pacific Opera Victoria puts on three operas a year at the McPherson and Royal theatres, including timeless masterpieces like *Madame Butterfly* and *The*

Far left: A scene from *Hansel and Gretel,* performed by the Vancouver Opera as part of its Opera in the Schools program. *Left:* Kokoro Dance's *Rage* is an extraordinary theatrical experience that combines dance, live music and film images to present a searing commentary on Canada's treatment of its citizens of Japanese ancestry during the Second World War.

Marriage of Figaro, as well as twentieth-century works such as *The Merry Widow.* The company also presents special programs for students from elementary school through university.

For more than three decades, the Vancouver Opera has presented four operas a year at the elegant Queen Elizabeth Theatre. The company performs classic works but in the 1993-94 season it staged a new Canadian opera entitled *The Architect.* The singers also perform mini-operas in elementary schools. A special high school program invites students to dress rehearsals and gives them a tour backstage.

Dance

Dance is alive and thriving in British Columbia. From September to June, Ballet B.C., under the direction of John Alleyne, stages bold, innovative works, which have included a dance set to popular love songs. The company has earned glowing reviews throughout Canada and the United States.

Choreographers such as Lola MacLaughlin, Karen Jamieson and Judith Marcuse present exciting, imaginative modern dance programs each year. Kokoro and Jumpstart dance companies also entertain dance enthusiasts with highly original and sometimes startling performances.

Canada's largest alternative dance festival, Dancing on the Edge, features new dancing from around the world. Over a two-week period, 60 to 70 shows are performed in every kind of setting, from traditional stages to the beautiful beaches of Vancouver.

Visual Arts

Many Native artists live and work in British Columbia. Bill Reid, a Haida artist living in Vancouver, makes carvings and sculptures out of wood, argillite, ivory and bronze. His luminous cedar sculpture entitled *Raven and the First Men,* showing the first people emerging from a clamshell, is on display in the Great Hall in Vancouver's

Left: Bill Reid's *Raven and the First Men. Far left:* The grizzly bear design in this button blanket by Florence Davidson was adapted from a nineteenth-century Haida tunic. Davidson is also the link in a long artistic tradition that began with her father, master carver Charles Edenshaw, and continues with her grandson Robert Davidson.

Museum of Anthropology. Reid also creates beautiful silver and gold jewellery, including tiny gold chests and masks that are worn as necklaces and pins.

On the Queen Charlotte Islands, Haida carver Rufus Moody works in argillite. This blue rock acquires a soft black shine when it is polished. Other well-known Native artists are Robert Davidson, who has carved totem poles for various places in Canada, and Tony Hunt, a Kwakiutl carver who learned his art from his father, Henry Hunt, and his grandfather, Mungo Martin. Native masks, totem poles, baskets, carvings and jewellery are displayed in shops, galleries and museums throughout British Columbia.

Many non-Native artists have been strongly influenced by Native art. Emily Carr, who was born in 1871, is probably British Columbia's most famous artist. She was deeply influenced by Native culture and by the mysterious beauty of the rain forests. The permanent collection of her work at the Vancouver Art Gallery is in great demand for exhibits overseas in places like China, where her art is highly prized and admired.

Emily Carr was associated with the famous Group of Seven in Toronto, who painted Canadian landscapes. Two members of this group, A.Y. Jackson and Lawren Harris, eventually settled in West

Right: Sign by Jack Shadbolt. *Far right: Indian Church,* a 1929 painting by Emily Carr

Vancouver. Another member, F.H. Varley, taught for ten years at the Vancouver School of Art.

One of Canada's pre-eminent painters today is Jack Shadbolt, who lives in Burnaby. His abstract paintings combining primitive and modern styles have inspired a generation of students. Like Carr, Shadbolt has been influenced by Native art.

Another famous B.C. artist is Toni Onley, who is known for his coastal scenes. Younger British Columbia artists who enjoy an international reputation are Jeff Wall and Kati Campbell. Using advertising techniques and forms, Jeff Wall creates gigantic photographic displays showing scenes that have a social message. Kati Campbell uses photographs to explore ideas about women's work and how we raise children.

Pottery and architecture are two other visual arts that are well represented on the coast. John Reeve, Wayne Ngan and Walter Dexter are highly admired potters. Arthur Erickson, Geoffrey Massey and the late Ron Thom have designed superlative buildings across the province and around the world.

Literature

Books are important to British Columbians, who buy more of them per capita than any other Canadians. There are about 230 publishing companies, including self-publishers, who are a growing force in the province. All told, B.C. publishers have approximately 2600 titles in print.

Poetry

Pauline Johnson, the daughter of a Mohawk chief and an Englishwoman, wrote poetry in the 1890s and early 1900s. Dressed in fringed buckskins, she toured Canada, the United States and Britain giving dramatic readings of her work. In 1901, she moved from Ontario to Vancouver, where she wrote stories based on Native folk tales.

Two well-known twentieth-century B.C. poets are Earle Birney and Dorothy Livesay. Both have won Governor General's awards for their work. Today Susan Musgrave, George Bowering and bill bissett are popular poets.

Prose

One of British Columbia's most admired fiction writers was Ethel Wilson, who wrote her first book in 1947 at age 59. Her most highly praised novel, *Swamp Angel*, tells the story of a woman who leaves her unhappy marriage in Vancouver for a fishing camp in the interior. A provincial park is named after Wilson.

Malcolm Lowry, author of the internationally acclaimed *Under the Volcano*, lived in British Columbia from 1940 to 1954. For a time his home was a shack on the beach near North Vancouver. It had no heat, electricity or plumbing. While living there, Lowry wrote a collection of short stories that won a Governor General's Award.

Important fiction writers today include Audrey Thomas, Jane Rule, crime writer L. R. (Bunny) Wright and science fiction writer William Gibson. Poet and novelist Joy Kogawa, who as a child during the Second World War was interned at a camp in the B.C.

interior along with thousands of other Japanese Canadians, wrote about this experience in her 1981 novel *Obasan*.

In recent years, several B.C. writers have enjoyed worldwide recognition. Douglas Coupland's books *Generation X, Shampoo Planet* and *Life After God* explore the lives of young adults living in the 1990s. Nick Bantock's beautiful *Griffin and Sabine* and its sequels, which he wrote and illustrated, follow a correspondence between two friends. The books were on the best-seller list for months.

British Columbians have also produced some of Canada's finest nonfiction. Artist Emily Carr won a Governor General's Award in 1941 for *Klee Wyck*, a collection of literary sketches. George Woodcock, one of Canada's leading men of letters, has published dozens of books, mostly works of literary criticism and political writings. A dedicated conservationist, Roderick Haig-Brown wrote numerous books containing his reflections on nature and on fishing, as well as several children's books and adult novels. Journalist Bruce Hutchison, who also wrote eloquently about nature and life in the country, was best known for his volumes of biography and history. Shuswap activist George Manuel wrote forcefully about the plight of his own people and indigenous people around the world.

Several of Canada's most popular children's authors live in British Columbia. Eric Wilson, who sets his series of mystery books in Canadian locations, lives in Victoria. Vancouver-based Kit Pearson won the Governor General's Award for *The Sky Is Falling*, and author-illustrator Ann Blades produced one of Canada's best-known picture books, *Mary of Mile 18*.

Recreation

British Columbia is a mecca for outdoor sports enthusiasts. With more than 5800 square kilometres (2240 square miles) of wilderness, several national parks and hundreds of provincial parks, there is something for everyone. People hike, camp, go horseback riding, bicycle and fish in rivers, lakes and the ocean. Hang-gliders soar with the eagles. Spelunkers explore underground caves the size of football fields, bristling with stalactites and stalagmites. In winter, many people enjoy downhill or cross-country skiing, and in the interior people ice fish. During the summer, water sports like swimming, kayaking, rafting, sailing, canoeing and scuba diving are very popular.

Organized sports are also popular in British Columbia. Games like soccer, cricket, ice hockey, football and baseball thrive throughout the province, as do lesser-known sports such as harness racing, kabaddi (Sikh wrestling) and rhythmic gymnastics. Local wheelchair athlete Rick Hansen has raised the profile of sporting events for the disabled.

Spectator Sports

Spectator sports are a major pastime in British Columbia. In cities and towns, amateur baseball, soccer, football and hockey teams compete in front of keen home-town crowds.

Vancouver's Empire Stadium was built in 1954 to host the British Empire Games and later became the home of the B.C. Lions football

Given the province's geography, it is not surprising that water sports and skiing are among British Columbians' favourite outdoor activities.

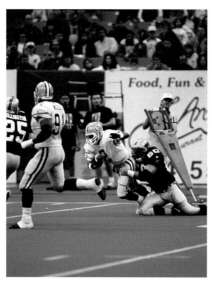

Right: The B.C. Lions (in black) in action against the Edmonton Eskimos. *Far right:* Vancouver Canucks star Pavel Bure in action

club. The Lions, who won the Grey Cup championship in 1964, moved their home games to B.C. Place Stadium in the 1980s.

In 1970, the Vancouver Canucks joined the National Hockey League. The Canucks have had several famous members. In particular, Pavel Bure, also known as the Russian Rocket, is a favourite among junior league hockey players.

Other Vancouver sports teams include the Vancouver Canadians AAA baseball team and the Vancouver 86ers, who play soccer at Swanguard Stadium in Burnaby.

Champions

British Columbia has had its share of sports champions. In 1928, sprinter Percy Williams won two Olympic gold medals, an achievement that remains unique in Canadian track and field history. Another famous B.C. sprinter, Harry Jerome, tied the world record for the 100-metre dash in 1960 and for the 100-yard dash in 1962. He also won a bronze medal in the 1954 Olympics and a gold medal in the 1967 Pan-American games.

Nancy Greene Raine is well known to British Columbians as the champion skier who won the World Cup in 1967 and again in 1968,

Far left: **Terry Fox, running in eastern Ontario during his Marathon of Hope.** *Left and above:* **Two B.C. champions: sprinter Harry Jerome and swimmer Elaine Tanner**

after winning Olympic gold in the giant slalom and silver in the slalom. She was also named Athlete of the Year in 1968.

Canada's best female swimmer ever was Elaine Tanner. She set world records in the 220-yard individual medley and the 200-yard butterfly in 1966, and that same year, at age 15, became the youngest person to receive the Lou Marsh Trophy as outstanding athlete of the year. In 1969, she received the Order of Canada.

There have been other B.C. champions — figure skater Karen Magnussen, rhythmic gymnast Lori Fung, wrestler Jeffrey Thue, to mention just a few — but no athlete ever aroused as much admiration as a young runner from Port Coquitlam who set no records and won no competitions. In 1980, after losing most of his right leg to bone cancer, Terry Fox set out to run across Canada to raise money for cancer research. He had completed two-thirds of his journey when the disease spread to his lungs and ended his personal Marathon of Hope. Over the next few months, his example inspired Canadians to donate almost $25 million to cancer research, and thousands still participate in the annual fund-raising runs that are held in his name.

CHAPTER 10

A Tour of British Columbia

The province advertises itself as "Super, Natural British Columbia," offering both cosmopolitan cities and rugged wilderness. Even in the cities, the wilderness is never far from anyone's doorstep.

The easiest way to appreciate this huge and varied province is by looking at its two most important cities and then at the nine main regions identified by the Department of Tourism.

Vancouver

Rimmed by mountains and ocean beaches, Vancouver boasts one of the most spectacular settings of any city in the world.

Stanley Park, home of the Vancouver Aquarium and the Stanley Park Zoo, is a 406-hectare (1000-acre) peninsula of tall cedars and landscaped gardens. The 10-kilometre (6.5-mile) sea wall surrounding the park is a popular pathway from which Vancouverites can watch the bustle of Vancouver Harbour — one of Canada's busiest and most important ports. Freighters from all over the world, gleaming white cruise ships travelling to and from Alaska, and oil tankers are all guided and pushed around by sturdy tug boats. Sea planes land and take off amid the shipping traffic. The tiny ferry known as the SeaBus scoots across Burrard Inlet, linking Vancouver and North Vancouver.

Stanley Park is not the only natural oasis in busy Vancouver. Pacific Spirit Park, once part of the University Endowment Lands

Clockwise from top: **The Vancouver Aquarium in Stanley Park; a spring stroll among Okanagan peach blossoms; rainforest trail in Pacific Rim National Park; summer tourists on Horstman Glacier, atop Blackcomb Mountain; night view of the Legislative Building, Victoria**

Top: The Lion's Gate Bridge connecting Vancouver to North Vancouver. *Bottom left:* Dr. Sun Yat-Sen Classical Chinese Garden. *Bottom right:* Gastown is Vancouver's oldest district. Vancouverites and visitors alike enjoy the nineteenth-century atmosphere provided by the cobblestone streets, old-fashioned lampposts and dozens of restored buildings that now house boutiques, antique shops, restaurants and art galleries.

of the University of British Columbia, is a 400-hectare (990-acre) woodland. Nearby on the university grounds, the Nitobe Memorial Gardens recreate a traditional Japanese garden.

Another of Vancouver's garden treasures is the Dr. Sun Yat-Sen Classical Chinese Garden in Chinatown. The only classical Chinese garden outside China, it was built using traditional Chinese methods and materials. Outside its walls, Vancouver's Chinatown, the second largest Chinatown in North America (after San Francisco), hums with activity. Just north and west of Chinatown is historic Gastown where Vancouver began. This area of old restored brick buildings and cobbled streets is named after John "Gassy Jack" Deighton, who built the first saloon here.

To learn more about Vancouver's history, visitors go to Vanier Park on the city's west side. The park is actually a museum complex that includes the Vancouver Museum, the H.R. MacMillan

Planetarium, the Gordon Southam Observatory, the Maritime Museum and the City of Vancouver Archives.

One of the most fascinating museums in Vancouver is the Museum of Anthropology at the University of British Columbia. This striking building was inspired by the traditional cedar houses of Northwest Coast Natives and contains one of the world's finest collections of their art. Natives are one of many cultural groups that give Vancouver its dynamic, cosmopolitan atmosphere. As a Pacific Rim city, it has strong traditional links with Asia through its thriving Chinese, Indian and Japanese communities. Its natural beauty, mild climate and diverse economy have attracted people from across Canada. This cultural mix has nurtured a vibrant artistic community.

Victoria

Located at the southern tip of Vancouver Island, the provincial capital, Victoria, is known as Canada's City of Flowers. The climate is so mild that flowers bloom year-round. Victorians take great pride in their annual Flower Count in February when they tell the rest of Canada how many millions of blossoms fill the city. Butchart Gardens, near Victoria, is one of Canada's most famous gardens.

Overlooking the city's inner harbour are the imposing Parliament Buildings and the magnificently restored Empress Hotel, for decades the heart of Victoria's social life. Many beautiful old brick buildings make the city's downtown attractive to both tourists and local citizens.

One of the best museums in Canada is located in Victoria. The Royal British Columbia Museum focuses on the province's natural and human history. Next to the museum, Thunderbird Park is filled with totem poles and a Native longhouse. Victoria's long naval history is celebrated at the Maritime Museum.

Greater Victoria includes the municipalities of Esquimalt, still an important naval base, Saanich and Oak Bay. North of Greater Victoria stretches the Saanich Peninsula, known for its fruit and

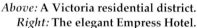
Above: **A Victoria residential district.**
Right: **The elegant Empress Hotel.**

vegetable farms, its dozens of beaches and Western Canada's oldest agricultural fair, held every September since 1871 at Saanichton.

Victoria and its neighbouring communities are isolated from the rest of the island by the high rocky ridge known as the Malahat. This ridge offers wonderful views of mainland mountains and of the Gulf Islands and the Saanich Peninsula.

Vancouver Island and the Gulf Islands

Once over the Malahat, travellers have easy access to the entire east coast of Vancouver Island. The west coast is not so easily accessible, however, because of the island's mountainous interior. Only two highways cross the island from east to west.

Just north of the Malahat is the Cowichan Valley and the city of Duncan. This is dairy farming and logging country. Known as "The City of Totems," Duncan celebrates its large Native population with over 60 totem poles and a Native Heritage Centre.

Farther north is the town of Chemainus, "The Little Town That Did." In the early 1980s, the citizens decided to keep their town alive through tourism after the local sawmill closed. They commissioned huge murals for the walls of the downtown

Top left: **The port of Nanaimo.** *Bottom left:* **Getting ready for the city's annual International Bathtub Race, which sees hundreds of variously powered bathtubs and other outlandish craft head out across the Strait of Georgia to Vancouver.** *Above:* **One of the famed Chemainus murals. Tourists can take walking tours to the 32 murals, following footprints on the sidewalks.**

buildings. The murals, showing scenes from the area's history, have made Chemainus an important tourist attraction.

The second-largest city on the island is Nanaimo, a rapidly growing retirement centre. Among the city's attractions are a picturesque waterfront, many well-preserved historic buildings, and some two dozen parks, which include bird sanctuaries and ancient Native stone carvings. At Parksville, also a growing retirement area, one of the cross-island highways begins. Along this road is the famous Cathedral Grove, a carefully preserved stand of old-growth forest. Some of the hundreds of Douglas firs here are over 800 years old.

The largest community in the island's interior is the logging town of Port Alberni. Although it is located in the middle, it is a port because it is situated at the head of long, narrow Alberni Inlet. From here, the small freighter M.V. *Lady Rose* travels to Bamfield and Ucluelet on the west coast, carrying supplies, mail and people.

The road west from Port Alberni becomes narrower and more

winding as it approaches the island's rugged west coast. The two communities here, Tofino and Ucluelet, rely on logging, fishing, and tourism. Tourists come here because of the wild beauty of Pacific Rim National Park, which includes Long Beach, the Broken Group Islands and the West Coast Trail.

North from Parksville on the east coast, Courtenay is located in the farming area of the Comox Valley. It provides access to the skiing areas of Forbidden Plateau and Mount Washington and to Strathcona Park. The highest peak on the island, the 2200-metre (7200-foot) Golden Hinde, is in the centre of the park, and Della Falls, the waterfall with the highest vertical drop in Canada (440 metres/1440 feet), is in the southern part of the park. The most northerly large community on Vancouver Island is Campbell River, a popular fishing resort as well as a logging and mining centre.

Between southern Vancouver Island and the mainland lie almost 200 islands of various shapes and sizes known as the Gulf Islands. Sheltered and dry, the islands are warm enough to grow cactus.

The largest Gulf Island is Saltspring. With its mix of mountains, gentle farmland, lakes, and ocean beaches, it attracts many visitors from the mainland and Vancouver Island. Because of its popularity, Saltspring is experiencing high land prices and rapid development.

The other popular islands are North and South Pender, Galiano and Mayne islands. The larger Gulf Islands are accessible from Vancouver Island and the mainland by regular ferry services.

Southwestern British Columbia

Southwestern British Columbia is a wedge stretching from the American border northwest up the Sunshine Coast and east into the interior of the province.

The most heavily populated part of the province is the Lower Mainland in the southwest corner. Here Vancouver and other cities and towns surround and cover the delta of the Fraser River. Due east of Vancouver is Burnaby, home to Simon Fraser University.

Due south, the city of Richmond is built on islands in the Fraser River delta. Southeast of Burnaby is "The Royal City" of New Westminster, British Columbia's first capital city. Nearby is Fort Langley National Historic Park where the Crown Colony of British Columbia was inaugurated in 1858. Surrey, located south of New Westminster, is the largest district municipality in the province and one of the fastest growing in Canada. There are some 60 parks in the Surrey area, as well as a marsh — the Serpentine Fen — that is home to more than 100 species of birds. North of Vancouver, on the north shore of Burrard Inlet, are the two large cities of North Vancouver and West Vancouver. Built on the lower slopes of the Coast Mountains, these cities get more rain than Vancouver because the mountains trap the clouds moving inland from the Pacific.

The highway leading west from West Vancouver passes through Horseshoe Bay where travellers can take a ferry to the aptly named Sunshine Coast. As well as an average 2000 hours of sunshine a year, this stretch of coast offers some of the world's best scuba diving. The largest community on the Sunshine Coast is Powell River with one of the world's biggest pulp and paper plants.

Swaying above North Vancouver's Capilano River is the Capilano Suspension Bridge, the longest and highest footbridge in the world. *Inset top:* Recreating life at a Hudson's Bay Company Post, Fort Langley National Historic Park. *Inset bottom:* Peace Arch Park is maintained jointly by British Columbia and the state of Washington. The arch itself straddles the Canada–U.S. border.

Instead of taking a ferry at Horseshoe Bay, travellers can continue north along the shore of Howe Sound through the town of Squamish. Above Squamish looms Stawamus Chief, a 762-metre (2500-foot) mountain that is a popular climbing and hiking spot. Beyond Squamish, the road climbs past the world-famous ski resorts of Whistler and Blackcomb to Mount Currie, a Native village surrounded by snow-capped mountains. In the 1860s, gold seekers trudged through this wilderness on their way to the Cariboo gold fields.

In the southern part of southwestern British Columbia lies the more tranquil countryside of the Fraser Valley. Dairy farms, market gardens and flower nurseries thrive in this lush green valley on the province's most fertile farmland. The largest communities in the valley are Abbotsford, Mission, Chilliwack and Hope.

Okanagan-Similkameen

The dry sunny climate of this region has made it a favourite of fruit farmers and tourists alike. The northern part of the Okanagan Valley is a dairy and vegetable-growing area. Vernon, at the head of Okanagan Lake, began as a commercial centre for the huge ranches in the area. The O'Keefe Historic Ranch offers a glimpse of these cattle empires of the past. Today Vernon is the business and tourist centre for the north Okanagan.

Kelowna is the largest city in the Okanagan. Its name means "grizzly bear" but no grizzly bears prowl the Okanagan today. The city is a commercial centre for the local orchards, canning plants, vineyards and wineries in and around it. With its sunny climate and pretty setting, it is a growing retirement centre.

The name of Penticton, at the foot of Okanagan Lake, means "place to stay forever." With its warm climate, beaches on two lakes and ski hills, the name suits the city. The southernmost city of the Okanagan-Similkameen is Osoyoos, close to the border with the United States and surrounded by desert. With heavy irrigation,

Far left: Campground on Osoyoos Lake, the warmest freshwater lake in Canada. *Left:* Historic O'Keefe Ranch, built about 1867. *Bottom left:* Statue of Ogopogo, the monster of Okanagan Lake. Tales of a fearsome lake monster have persisted since long before European settlers came to the area.

farmers have made the desert a rich orchard area that produces some of the earliest fruits in Canada.

The Similkameen River Valley in the southwest is a traditional mining area that had its own gold rush in the 1890s. The area is rich in copper, gold and other metals. Mining continues, but agriculture, tourism and logging are also important to the economy.

Kootenay Country

Born of many mining booms, Kootenay Country, east of the Okanagan, is a mix of snow-capped mountains and green valleys.

Castlegar is known locally as the "Crossroads of the Kootenays." Doukhobors settled here in the early 1900s, and their culture is showcased in the local Doukhobor Historical Museum. Trail is a major mining centre with a large smelter, and Rossland is an old gold town. At the turn of the century, Rossland was the province's fourth-largest city, producing half of its gold. Today "prospectors" can visit the LeRoi Gold Mine at the Rossland Museum, the only hardrock gold mine in Canada open to the public.

The city of Nelson is nestled on the West Arm of Kootenay Lake in the heart of the Selkirk Mountains. Nelson is called the "Heritage

Above: Kootenay Country is mining country. Most of the ore extracted in the area is processed at Trail, seen here on a winter evening. *Right:* The S.S. *Moyie,* now permanently anchored at Kaslo, was one of a whole fleet of sternwheelers that once plied Kootenay Lake.

Capital of the Kootenays" because of the 350 turn-of-the-century buildings that date from its mining heyday.

Kootenay Country is hot springs country. At Nakusp in the northern part of the region and at Ainsworth Hot Springs, on Kootenay Lake, visitors can soak in hot, mineralized waters year-round. At Kaslo on Kootenay Lake, the S.S. *Moyie,* last of the sternwheelers that brought supplies and people to pioneer settlements before the railway and good roads were built, is now a museum. It was retired in 1957 after 60 years of service.

Rocky Mountains

The Rocky Mountains region of British Columbia lies in its southeast corner along the border with Alberta. Over half the province's elk population lives in this area, which is also a major migration route for birds travelling the Columbia River flyway.

The Rocky Mountains region is home to three of the six national parks located in British Columbia. Glacier National Park contains over 400 glaciers. With one of the heaviest snowfalls in the world, Rogers Pass in the park is the site of the world's largest avalanche control program. Yoho National Park gets its name from the Cree word meaning "how magnificent." Kootenay National Park,

Left: A clear mountain lake provides a perfect reflection of the granite spires of the Bugaboo Range. *Above:* A few of the restored buildings at Fort Steele, named for Major Sam Steele, who established B.C.'s first North-West Mounted Police post nearby in 1887.

bordering on the southeast portion of Yoho, is actually the floor of an ancient ocean. It was established to protect the area's many canyons, mineral hot springs and waterfalls.

From here the road leads south to Kimberley, Cranbrook and Fort Steele. Kimberley is known as the "Bavarian City of the Canadian Rockies" and looks like a village in southern Germany. There is a fine Railway Museum in Cranbook. Nearby, at Fort Steele, 60 restored buildings and costumed townspeople recreate the community's gold-mining past.

High Country

British Columbia's High Country, with its lakes, turbulent rivers and rolling rangeland, juts southwest from the mountains of the Alberta border through the houseboating waters of Shuswap Lake to the ranch country of Douglas Lake.

The region includes Mount Robson Provincial Park, Wells Gray Provincial Park and Mount Revelstoke National Park. Mount Robson (3977 metres/13 048 feet) is the highest peak in the Canadian Rockies. Wells Gray Provincial Park contains a dozen large waterfalls and an extinct volcano.

In Monck Provincial Park, on the north shore of Nicola Lake, are the remains of a *kikuli* (pit house), the winter dwelling used by the Interior Salish and Athapaskan peoples.

Shuswap Lake is a popular summer resort area because of its sandy beaches and protected anchorages. The Adams River, which flows into Shuswap Lake, is famous for its fish. Every four years (1994, 1998, 2002, and so forth), a "dominant" sockeye salmon run fills the river, turning the waters blood red as crimson salmon head for their spawning grounds. The largest community in the High Country is the city of Kamloops, which lies where the North and South Thompson rivers meet. It began as a fur-trading post in the early 1800s and is now a forestry, mining, ranching and tourism centre. Its name means "meeting place."

Cariboo-Chilcotin

Rolling from east to west almost clear across the province, the wild, untamed Cariboo-Chilcotin is British Columbia's "true west." Here, under wide blue skies, some of Canada's largest ranches spread across the high plateau. The snow-covered peaks of the Coast and Cariboo mountain ranges dominate the region.

Clockwise from top left: Float plane at the Monarch Ice Fields near Tweedsmuir Provincial Park, one of the most varied wilderness areas in Canada; small town rodeo; whitewater rafting in Wells Gray Provincial Park; marina near Salmon Arm at the southern end of Shuswap Lake

The Cariboo to the east and the Chilcotin to the west each has its own unique character. The communities of the Cariboo were shaped by the historic gold rush that began in 1858. Quesnel, the area's largest town, developed as a supply centre for the gold miners. At Barkerville Historic Park, restored and reconstructed buildings give visitors a taste of a real gold rush town.

From Williams Lake west to the Coast Mountains is the cowboy country of the Chilcotin. Cattle from these rangelands are sent to markets across Canada. On the western edge of the plateau, Tweedsmuir Provincial Park offers a widely varied wilderness that includes glaciers, alpine meadows and grassy valleys.

Far to the west is the coastal community of Bella Coola, separated from the rest of the province by the Coast Mountains. The road into the community was built only in the 1950s when the residents completed it themselves rather than wait for the government to do it. The communities of Ocean Falls and Bella Bella are even more remote and can be reached only by water or air.

Northwest

Home to the legendary Klondike Gold Rush Trail, the Tatshenshini River and totem poles, the Northwest region of British Columbia is a vast L-shaped wilderness. It stretches from the Rockies in the east to the Queen Charlotte Islands and Alaska in the west, and from Cariboo Country to the Yukon border.

The mist-cloaked Queen Charlotte Islands are the homeland of the Haida people, whose name for them is Haida Gwaii. The remains of ancient Haida villages are scattered throughout the dense rain forest along the islands' coasts. Today, the Haida are not the only residents of the islands. Natives and non-Natives work in the fishing, logging, mining and tourism industries.

Prince Rupert, built on an island near the mouth of the Skeena River, is the second most-important port in the province, and it is the commercial and transportation centre for the northwest.

Southeast of Prince Rupert is the "aluminum city" of Kitimat. A huge aluminum smelter built here in the 1950s has been joined by a large methanol plant. This modern industrial city is surrounded by wilderness. A single road leads north to Terrace, named for the terraced bank from which it overlooks the Skeena.

Human history is an important attraction in this region. Kitwanga Fort National Historic Site was part of a Native trading network and the location of several famous Native battles. At the village of Kitwancool is the oldest standing totem pole in the world, known as "Hole-through-the Ice." Nearby at Hazelton, the 'Ksan Indian Village recreates a Gitksan community that stood at the junction of the Bulkley and Skeena rivers until the 1870s. Six longhouses are decorated with carved poles and painted fronts.

In the eastern part of the region, visitors can explore a Hudson's Bay fort of the late 1800s at Fort St. James National Historic Site. The village of Fort St. James is the oldest non-Native community in the province. To the south, Vanderhoof is the geographical centre of British Columbia. The largest city in northern British Columbia is Prince George, located where the Nechako and Fraser rivers meet. Today it is a major commercial and transportation centre and home of the new University of Northern British Columbia.

Below: **Farm near McBride.** *Right:* **Totem poles at Kispiox, in the Hazelton area**

Atlin, the main centre of the extreme northwest, sits beside a turquoise lake, backed by snow-clad mountains. Due west of Atlin lies the legendary Klondike Gold Rush Trail. Miners' gear litters the trail and is protected from vandalism by law.

Peace River

Explorer Alexander Mackenzie called the Peace River region a "magnificent theatre of nature" because of its mountains, powerful rivers and rolling grasslands. Today this region has fields of grain, huge hydroelectric dams, mines and oil wells.

From Mile 0 at Dawson Creek on the southeast edge of the region, the Alaska Highway winds northwest to the Yukon border and beyond. A popular tourist route in summer, the highway is also an important supply route for northern communities.

Northwest of Dawson Creek, Fort St. John is the largest community north of Prince George. The first oil well in British Columbia was drilled near here. Fort Nelson, farther north, is also an important centre for petroleum and natural gas development.

The largest "lake" in the province is in the southwest corner of the region — Williston Lake, formed when the W.A.C. Bennett Dam was built.

Far left: **Harvesting barley in the Peace River Valley.**
Left: **Dawson Creek signpost marking the beginning of the Alaska Highway**

Facts
at a Glance

General Information

Provincehood: July 20, 1871

Origin of Name: Queen Victoria suggested the name of British Columbia for the colony that had existed since 1858.

Provincial Capital: Victoria

Provincial Nickname: The Pacific Province

Provincial Flag: The upper part of the flag is a Union Jack with a golden crown in the centre. This symbolizes the province's origins as a British colony. The lower part shows a golden half sun superimposed over three wavy blue bars that represent the Pacific Ocean. The sun setting over the ocean is symbolic of British Columbia's position as Canada's most westerly province.

Motto: *Splendor Sine Occasu:* The Latin words are translated "Splendour without diminishment."

Provincial Flower: Pacific dogwood

Provincial Bird: Steller's jay

Provincial Tree: Western red cedar

Provincial Mineral: Jade

Population

(1991 census)

Population: 3 282 061

Population Density: 3.7 people per km^2 (9.58 per sq. mi.)

Population Distribution: 55.8% of British Columbians live on 4.2% of the land area in the southwestern corner of the province.

Greater Vancouver	1 542 744
Greater Victoria	299 550
Kelowna	75 950
Prince George	69 653
Kamloops	67 057
Nanaimo	60 129

Population Growth: British Columbia is Canada's fastest-growing province.

1871	36 247
1881	49 459
1891	98 173
1901	178 657
1911	392 480
1931	694 263
1941	817 861
1951	1 165 210
1961	1 629 082
1971	2 184 600
1981	2 713 615
1991	3 282 061

Geography

Borders: British Columbia lies between the 49th and 60th northern parallels of latitude and between the 120th and 144th meridians of longitude. It is bordered by the

American states of Washington, Idaho and Montana on the south, and Alaska on the northwest, by Alberta on the east and by the Yukon and Northwest Territories on the north.

Highest Point: Fairweather Mountain (on the border with Alaska), 4663 m (15 300 ft.). Mount Waddington, 4106 m (13 175 ft.), is the highest point entirely within the province.

Lowest Point: Sea level along the coast

Area: 948 596 km^2 (366 281 sq. mi.) of which about 2% is fresh water

Rank in Area Among Provinces: Third

Time Zone: Most of B.C. is on Pacific Time; the Peace River region and the Kootenays are on Mountain Time.

National and Provincial Parks: British Columbia's spectacular natural beauty is protected in six national parks (Gwaii Haanas, Pacific Rim, Mount Revelstoke, Kootenay, Yoho and Glacier) and over 400 provincial parks and recreation areas.

Rivers: Rivers draining into the Pacific Ocean include the Fraser, Skeena, Stikine, Nass and (via Oregon) the Columbia. The Liard and the Peace rivers drain eventually into the Arctic Ocean.

Lakes: British Columbia has thousands of lakes. The largest are Williston, Nechacko and Upper and Lower Arrow lakes formed behind dams. Atlin, Babine, Kootenay, Stuart and Okanagan are the largest natural lakes.

Topography: British Columbia is a sea of mountains, interspersed with plateaus, plains and lowlands. The major mountain ranges are: the Coast, Skeena, Cascade, Cassiar, Omineca, Cariboo, Monashee, Selkirk, Purcell and Rocky Mountains. The northeastern corner of the province is an extension of the high plains of western Alberta. The southwestern corner is a flat lowland formed by the delta of the Fraser River. The biggest offshore islands are Vancouver Island and Graham and Moresby islands in the Queen Charlottes.

Climate: Moisture-laden clouds from the Pacific Ocean rise when they meet the mountains, and the moisture in them condenses to form rain. As a result, rainfall on the west side of the mountains tends to be greater than on the east. Vancouver Island's climate is mild because of the Pacific Ocean. In Victoria, the average January and July temperatures are 4.1°C (39.3°F) and 15.4°C (60°F), respectively. Winters on the mainland coast are generally mild and wet. In the interior they are colder, and summers are hotter. In Princeton, the average January temperature is -8°C (17°F), and the average July temperature is 18°C (65°F). Although very little snow falls at the lower elevations along the coast, snow is an expected part of B.C. winters at higher coastal elevations and in the interior.

Nature

Trees: About 60% of the province is covered with forests. Important trees include Douglas fir, western red cedar, hemlock, Sitka spruce, western red pine, lodgepole pine, balsam fir, poplar, Garry oak, and birch.

Wild Plants: B.C. is home to hundreds of varieties of wild plants. These include various kinds of grasses, mosses, ferns and lichens, mushrooms, sedges, wildflowers and wild berries.

Animals: The 112 species of mammals in the province include grizzly bear, cougar, mountain goat, bighorn sheep, moose, black-tailed deer, elk, hoary marmot, Townsend vole, pika, orca, grey and humpback whales, seals, sea otters, and sea lions. Fifteen species of reptiles and 19 species of amphibians are found here.

Birds: Among the hundreds of bird species are 266 species of water birds, including ducks, pelicans, herons, swans and geese; and 34 species of raptors, such as ospreys and hawks. Other species include rufous hummingbirds, whiskey jacks and rhinoceros auklets. Twenty-eight of the bird species found in B.C. are endangered, threatened or of special concern.

Fish: Five species of salmon, lingcod, halibut, rainbow, brown and cutthroat trout, steelhead and Dolly Varden are the main fish species.

Young grizzly bear

Commons and five seats in the Senate. Provincial laws are passed by an elected single-chamber Legislative Assembly of 75 members. Municipalities of various kinds are responsible for local government services. The province has 41 cities, 14 towns, 44 villages, 51 district municipalities, 29 regional districts and 300 improvement districts.

The Courts: British Columbia has a three-tiered court system. At the first, or lowest, level is the Provincial Court, which hears most of the criminal cases. At the second level is the Supreme Court of British Columbia, which hears civil cases as well as very serious criminal cases. At the highest level is the Appeal Court of British Columbia. This court hears matters appealed from the decisions of lower courts.

Government and the Courts

Governments: British Columbia has 32 seats in the federal House of

Education

Seventy-five local school districts administer public school education. Education is offered from kindergarten through to grade 12. In 1992, the province's 1599 public schools enrolled 527 000 pupils, while 246 independent schools enrolled 37 000 pupils. The language of instruction in most schools is English. Various French programs are available in many areas, and other languages such as Japanese, Chinese, Spanish and German are also taught.

A number of post-secondary programs are offered at 15 community colleges and 3 institutes located throughout the province. During 1991-1992, 43 000 full-time and 39 000 part-time students took courses.

Four university colleges, located in Kamloops, Chilliwak, Nanaimo and Kelowna, offer courses leading to bachelor degrees. Four publicly funded universities offer a wide range of undergraduate, graduate and professional programs: the University of British Columbia in Vancouver, Simon Fraser University in Burnaby, the University of Victoria in Victoria and the University of Northern British Columbia in Prince George. There is also one privately funded university. In 1992, approximately 42 000 full-time and 20 000 part-time students were enrolled in university programs.

Economy and Industry

British Columbia's economy is based on natural resource extraction, manufacturing and service industries. In 1991, the provincial Gross Domestic Product (GDP) was $73.9 million. Service-producing industries such as finance, transportation, and public administration generated 72.2% of the total GDP. Goods-producing industries generated the rest.

Primary Products

Wood: B.C. lumber, newsprint, pulp and paper, shingles and shakes are in demand throughout the world. Forest-industry shipments totalled $10.2 billion in 1991, representing 44.2% of all manufacturing shipments.

Minerals: Mines produce copper, gold, silver, lead, zinc, molybdenum, asbestos, sulphur and coal. Mineral production totalled $3.5 billion in 1991, with copper accounting for the largest share.

Energy: The energy industry produces coal, hydroelectricity, oil and natural gas. The total value of coal production in 1991 was $949 million. The total value of oil and gas production was $817 million. Some hydroelectricity, some natural gas and almost all of the coal produced were exported.

Agriculture: B.C. ranks sixth among the provinces in farm earnings, which were estimated at $1.23 billion during 1991. Farm holdings cover 2.4 million ha (6 million acres).

Fish: More than 40 species of fish and marine animals are harvested and marketed by the province's fishing and aquaculture industries. There are 240 fish-processing plants on the coast and a fishing fleet of 6200 vessels. In 1991, exports of fish and seafood products were valued at $635 million.

Secondary Products and Services

Manufacturing: Manufacturing shipments, made up mainly of petroleum products and food products, were valued at $23 billion in 1991. Other products included metal and chemical goods, computer technology, communications equipment and clothing.

Tourism: In 1991, British Columbia residents and visitors made over 23 million overnight trips in the province. Countless excursionists also took one-day trips. These travellers helped create tens of thousands of jobs and generated $5.5 billion.

Transportation: All B.C. ports are ice-free year-round. In 1990, the Port of Vancouver handled $38.75 billion in goods. The BC Ferry Corporation has 27 routes between the Lower Mainland, Vancouver Island and coastal ports. In 1990-1992, it carried almost 20 million passengers and over 7 million vehicles. The province has 6800 km (4225 mi.) of railway track. Vancouver International is the province's largest airport. It handles 10 million passengers a year and is served by major Canadian and international airlines. B.C.'s highway network is made up of 20 554 km (12 772 mi.) of paved roads, 21 388 km (13 290 mi.) of unpaved roads and 2677 bridges.

Communications: British Columbia has 87 originating radio stations and 10 originating television stations. There are 17 daily newspapers and 160 weekly or community newspapers, some of which publish in languages other than English. There are over 230 book publishers.

Social and Cultural Life

Museums and Art Galleries: British Columbia has about 190 museums. Some, like the Royal British Columbia Museum in Victoria, are internationally renowned. Others, like the tiny museum in the former jail at Miner's Bay on Mayne Island, are much smaller and are not well known outside the area.

In Vancouver, important museums include the Museum of Anthropology, the H.R. MacMillan Planetarium and the Vancouver Museum. The maritime

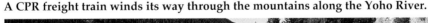

A CPR freight train winds its way through the mountains along the Yoho River.

museums in both Vancouver and Victoria are well worth visiting. Other museums of interest are the mining exhibits at Britannia and Rossland, the Burnaby Village Museum, the British Columbia Forest Museum near Duncan and the Museum of Northern British Columbia in Prince George.

The work of prominent artists is displayed in galleries such as the Emily Carr Gallery in Victoria, the Kamloops Public Art Gallery and the Vancouver Art Gallery.

Notable among museums devoted to Native art are 'Ksan at Hazelton, the Kwakiutl Museum in Cape Mudge Village on Quadra Island and the U'Mista Cultural Centre at Alert Bay.

Festivals: Countless festivals take place around the province.

On Vancouver Island, summer music festivals include the Victoria Folkfest and Jazz Festival, the Choirfest in Port Alberni and the Bluegrass Festival in Coombs.

In Vancouver, the festival season begins with the Children's Festival and continues with the International Dragon Boat Festival, the Diwali Festival of Lights, the Vancouver Sea Festival, and the International Writers and Readers Festival.

Festivals held elsewhere in southwestern British Columbia include the Salmon Festival in Steveston, the Seabird Island Indian Festival in Harrison Hot Springs and the Agassiz Fall Fair and Corn Festival.

In the Okanagan, the Penticton Peach Festival and the Osoyoos Cherry Fiesta Parade take place in July, and the Okanagan Wine Festival is celebrated throughout the region in the fall. Festivals in the Kootenays, the Rockies and the Cariboo include the Sunfest in Castlegar, Sam Steele Days in Cranbrook and the Williams Lake Stampede. Up north, Prince Rupert celebrates Seafest, and Prince George hosts Simon Fraser Days.

Performing Arts: There are several large theatres in Vancouver and Victoria and smaller ones across the province. British Columbians enjoy performances by the Vancouver- and Victoria-based symphony orchestras, choirs, and opera companies, as well as by such prominent dance companies as Ballet B.C. and the Judith Marcuse Dance Company.

Sports: Fans can cheer National Hockey League action with the Vancouver Canucks, football with the B.C. Lions Football Team, baseball with the Vancouver Canadians and soccer with the Vancouver 86ers. There is also plenty of minor league hockey, intercollegiate basketball, volleyball and World Cup downhill skiing.

Historic Sites and Landmarks

Barkerville Historic Park is a restored village from the Cariboo Gold Rush of the 1800s. Open year-round, it comes alive in summer with re-enactments of gold-rush life.

Doukhobor Heritage Village in Castlegar offers a glimpse of the culture of the Doukhobor immigrants

Gold rush days recreated at historic Barkerville

who settled this area in 1908. The tomb of their leader Peter Verigin is nearby.

Fort Langley National Historic Site is the official birthplace of British Columbia. Founded in 1827, the fort was the site of the proclamation of the colony of British Columbia in 1858.

Fort Steele, near Cranbrook, grew during the 1864 Kootenay Gold Rush. Sixty restored buildings allow visitors to experience life in a turn-of-the-century town.

Fort St. James National Historic Park recreates the atmosphere of a frontier trading post. The fort was founded in 1806 by Simon Fraser.

Provincial Legislature, in Victoria, was designed by Francis Rattenbury and completed in 1897. It overlooks Victoria's beautiful inner harbour.

West Coast Trail was established along the southwestern coast of Vancouver Island in 1907 to help shipwrecked sailors reach coastal communities. Now it is an internationally famous hiking trail.

Other Interesting Places to Visit

Botanical Beach, on the west coast of Vancouver Island, is famous for its tidal pools and huge variety of marine life, including chitons, sea robins, urchins and sea anemones.

Chinatown in Vancouver is a vibrant, 100-year-old community with many intriguing shops and restaurants.

Fisgard Lighthouse National Historical Site is at the entrance to Esquimalt Harbour. Built in 1860, the lighthouse was operated for 68 years.

Ninstints, the abandoned Haida village on Anthony Island in the Queen Charlotte Islands is a UNESCO World Heritage Site. It contains the largest number of original-standing totem poles in the world.

O'Keefe Historic Ranch, established in 1867, was one of the earliest cattle ranches developed in the Okanagan. Today it includes a furnished log house, a working blacksmith's shop and St. Ann's, the oldest Catholic church in the interior.

Sasquatch Provincial Park is named for the huge ape-like creature that is said to roam the densely wooded shores of Harrison Lake. The lake itself is famous for its hot springs.

Stanley Park in Vancouver is one of the largest inner-city parks in North America. It is a mix of forests, manicured lawns and attractions such as the zoo, the aquarium and the seawall walkway.

Important Dates

Thousands of years before specific events can be dated, the ancestors of today's Native people had established themselves in the lands now known as British Columbia.

1774   Spanish expedition under Juan José Pérez Hernández reaches the Queen Charlotte Islands and anchors later in Nootka Sound.

1778   Captain James Cook lands at Nootka Sound.

1792-   Captain George Vancouver
1794   surveys the coastline.

1793   Alexander Mackenzie reaches the Pacific coast by travelling overland from Lake Athabasca.

1805   Simon Fraser builds the first of several trading posts in the central interior.

1807-   David Thompson explores
1812   and maps much of the Columbia River area.

1808   Fraser reaches the Pacific Ocean by travelling down the Fraser River.

1827   The Hudson's Bay Company completes construction of Fort Langley.

1835-   Smallpox epidemics sweep
1838   the northwest coast and many Native people die.

1843   Construction of Fort Victoria begins under Chief Factor James Douglas.

1846   The Oregon Boundary Treaty establishes the 49th parallel as the land border between American and British territory west of the Rocky Mountains.

1849   Vancouver Island becomes a Crown colony.

1851   James Douglas is appointed governor of Vancouver Island.

1858   The Fraser River Gold Rush begins; the B.C. mainland becomes a Crown colony.

1859   New Westminster becomes the mainland capital.

1861   Mining boom begins in the Cariboo; construction begins on the Cariboo Wagon Road.

1862   Smallpox epidemic devastates the Native population.

1866   B.C. mainland and Vancouver Island are united.

1868   Victoria is chosen as the capital of the United Colony of British Columbia.

1870   The first canned salmon is exported from B.C.

1871   British Columbia joins Confederation.

1877   Coal miners strike on Vancouver Island.

1880   Canadian Pacific Railway (CPR) construction begins.

1885   CPR is completed; the "last spike" is pounded in at Craigellachie.

1886   Vancouver is selected as the terminus of CPR; Yoho and Glacier are established as the first national parks.

1888   Stanley Park in Vancouver officially opens.

1890   The Red Mountain mineral discovery triggers the West Kootenay mining boom.

1907   Anti-Oriental riots break out in Vancouver.

1911   Strathcona Park becomes the first provincial B.C. park.

1912	Coal miners on Vancouver Island begin a two-year strike.
1913	Hell's Gate landslides block the Fraser River and affect salmon spawning.
1914	Sikh passengers on the *Komagata Maru* are not allowed to disembark in Vancouver; the First World War begins; the Grand Trunk Railway (now CNR) completes its line into Prince Rupert.
1917	B.C. women gain the provincial vote.
1919	The Winnipeg General Strike is followed by sympathy strikes in B.C.
1929	The Great Depression begins.
1938	Jobless men riot in Vancouver.
1939	World War II begins.
1942	Japanese British Columbians are evacuated from the west coast and interned.
1943	The Alaska Highway is completed.
1947	Chinese and East Indians are allowed to vote in federal and provincial elections.
1949	Native people are allowed to vote in provincial elections; Japanese are allowed to return to the west coast and to vote in provincial and federal elections.
1952	W.A.C. Bennett leads Social Credit Party to its first B.C. victory.
1954	Vancouver hosts the British Empire Games.
1960	Native people are allowed to vote in federal elections.
1962	The B.C. portion of the Trans-Canada Highway is completed.
1964	The Columbia River Treaty is signed by the United States and Canada; joint development of hydroelectric power on the Columbia River follows.
1972	The New Democratic Party (NDP) comes to power for the first time in B.C.; Dave Barrett becomes premier.
1975	Social Credit leader Bill Bennett becomes premier.
1986	Expo 86 World's Fair takes place in Vancouver; Social Credit leader Bill Vander Zalm becomes premier.
1988	The federal government officially apologizes to Japanese British Columbians interned during World War II.
1990	The provincial government agrees to participate in Native land claims negotiations.
1991	Social Credit leader Rita Johnston becomes the first woman premier; the NDP under Mike Harcourt is elected.

B.C. Place during Expo 86

Sir Matthew Begbie

W.A.C. Bennett

Earle Birney

Frank Calder

Important People

Bryan Adams (1959-), born in Ontario; husky-voiced singer, songwriter, rock star; achieved international fame with such albums as *Cuts Like a Knife* and *Waking Up the Neighbors*; also performs in concerts for social and political causes

David Barrett (1930-), born in Vancouver; social worker, politician; NDP leader, 1970-83; as premier, 1972-75, instituted many social reforms; federal MP, 1988-93

Robert Bateman (1930-), born in Ontario; artist, teacher; has achieved international fame with finely detailed, realistic wildlife paintings

Sir Matthew Baillie Begbie (1819-1894), born at sea to British parents; first B.C. judge; sent from England to preserve law and order during the gold rush; upheld the rights of Native people and Chinese residents; was also the province's first chief justice

William Andrew Cecil Bennett (1900-1979); politician; came to Kelowna in 1930; leader of the new Social Credit Party; premier, 1952-72, during an era of explosive growth; succeeded as party leader by his son **William (Bill),** who was premier, 1975-86

Thomas Berger (1933-), born in Victoria; lawyer, judge, politician, civil libertarian; known for his strong support of aboriginal land claims and for heading the inquiry that recommended against building a pipeline through the Mackenzie Valley

Earle Birney (1904-), born in Calgary; writer; published more than 20 volumes of poetry, work has been translated into a dozen languages; has given more than 1500 poetry readings in 30 countries; won two Governor General's awards

Pavel Bure (1971-), born in Moscow; hockey player; became famous at age 21 as right-winger for the Canucks

Frank Calder (1915-), born at Nass Harbour; served as MLA for 26 years; was the first Native person to be elected to a provincial legislature; appointed Minister of the Crown in Canada (1972-73); known for the 1973 Calder case, a landmark decision on the Nishga land claims in the Supreme Court of Canada

Kim Campbell (1947-), born in Port Alberni; politician; MLA, 1986-88, MP, 1988-93; held several cabinet posts before becoming the first woman and the first British Columbian to serve as prime minister of Canada (June-October 1993)

Emily Carr (1871-1945), born in Victoria; painter, writer;

travelled to remote parts of the west coast to paint the wild forests, Native villages and totem poles; now recognized as one of Canada's greatest artists; wrote *Klee Wyck* (Governor General's Award), *The Book of Small, The House of All Sorts*

Brent Carver (1951-), born in Cranbrook; actor, comic, singer; known for his one-man shows and roles in rock operas; won Tony Award for his performance in *Kiss of the Spider Woman*

Amor De Cosmos (1825-1897), born William Alexander Smith in Nova Scotia; journalist, politician, premier, 1872-74; arrived in Victoria in 1858, founded the *British Colonist* newspaper; represented Victoria at four levels of government; strong supporter of Confederation

Robert Davidson (1946-), born in Alaska into Haida Eagle clan; great-grandson of master carver Charles Edenshaw; sculptor, printmaker, jeweller; uses traditional Haida shapes and symbols in a modern way

Sir James Douglas (1803-1877), born in British Guiana (now Guyana); trader, governor; founded Fort Victoria in 1843 while chief factor of Hudson's Bay Company; named governor of Vancouver Island in 1851 and of British Columbia in 1858; often called "the Father of British Columbia"

Robert Dunsmuir (1825-1889), Scottish-born coal baron; came to B.C. in 1851; discovered a rich coal seam north of Nanaimo in 1869, opened his own mine and was soon known as the coal king of B.C.; disliked by miners because of his disregard for safety and ruthless anti-union stands. His son **James Dunsmuir** (1851-1920) ruled the family business empire for many years and served briefly as premier and later as lieutenant-governor

Arthur Erickson (1924-), born in Vancouver; architect; designed many of Canada's greatest public buildings, including the Museum of Anthropology at UBC, Simon Fraser University and Roy Thomson Hall in Toronto; also designed the Canadian Embassy in Washington, D.C.

Judith Forst (1943-), born in New Westminster, one of the world's top mezzo-sopranos; has sung with famous opera companies all over the world; named Canadian Woman of the Year, 1978

Seraphim ("Joe") Fortes (?-1922), born in Barbados, came to Vancouver in 1885; as lifeguard at English Bay performed more than 100 rescues and taught thousands of Vancouver children to swim; children's drinking fountain at English Bay erected in his honour in 1927

Terry Fox (1958-1981), born in Manitoba, raised in Port

Kim Campbell

Emily Carr

Amor De Cosmos

Judith Forst

Chief Dan George

Nancy Greene Raine

Rick Hansen

Harry Jerome

Coquitlam; athlete; in 1980 on an artificial right leg ran across Canada to raise money for cancer research; his "Marathon of Hope" raised $25 million, and fund-raising runs are still held each year in his name

Chief Dan George (1899-1981), born on Burrard Reserve; actor, writer; chief of Squamish Band, 1951-63; began acting at age 60 and became famous in movies such as *Little Big Man;* wrote two volumes of prose poems; respected as a wise and gentle Native elder

Dorothy Grant (1955-), born in Alaska into Haida Raven clan; fashion designer; uses Native designs in high fashion clothes ("wearable art"); her designs are in art collections around the world

Nancy Greene Raine (1943-), raised in Rossland; athlete; member of national ski team, 1959-68; won the 1967 and 1968 World Cups and gold and silver medals at 1968 Olympics; won the Lou Marsh Trophy for Athlete of the Year (1967, 1968); named B.C. Female of the Half-Century

Helena Gutteridge (1879-1960), suffragist, union official, politician; played a leading role in B.C. women's fight for the vote; in 1937, became the first woman elected to Vancouver City Council

Roderick Haig-Brown (1908-1976); conservationist, writer; his love of fishing and his concern for the environment are subjects for many of his 25 books; won Governor General's Award for *Saltwater Summer*

Rick Hansen (1957-), born in Port Alberni; athlete; won 19 international wheelchair marathons and was world champion three times; on his 1985-87 "Man in Motion Tour," wheeled 40 000 kilometres (25 000 miles) and raised $20 million for spinal cord research and wheelchair sports

Bruce Hutchison (1901-1992), raised in Victoria; journalist, author; considered one of Canada's best writers about the West; his best-known book is probably *The Unknown Country;* won three Governor General's awards

Harry Jerome (1940-1982), raised in Vancouver; athlete; one of the greatest sprinters Canada has produced; held world records in the 1960s and won a bronze medal at the 1964 Olympics; statue erected in Stanley Park in his honour

Joy Kogawa (1935-), born in Vancouver; writer; during Second World War was sent to internment camp for Japanese Canadians in Slocan; her novel *Obasan* tells the story of this experience

Kwah (1755?-1840), born near Fort St. James; Carrier chief; provided food and guidance to Simon Fraser and European fur traders; said to have saved the life of James Douglas

David See-Chai Lam (1923-), born in Hong Kong; philanthropist; moved to Vancouver in 1967 and was successful in real estate; made important gifts to B.C. educational and cultural institutions; appointed lieutenant-governor in 1988

Dorothy Livesay (1909-), born in Manitoba, lives on Galiano Island; poet, reporter, teacher; has won many poetry prizes, including Governor General's Award for *Day and Night,* a book of poems on social themes

Sir Richard McBride (1870-1917), born in New Westminster; politician; elected to the B.C. Legislature in 1898; premier from 1903 to 1915, during a period of industrial expansion and prosperity; after resigning, become agent-general for B.C. in London, England

Helen Gregory MacGill (1864-1947), feminist, reformer, judge; first woman to graduate from the University of Toronto; moved to Vancouver in 1903; worked for 40 years to improve the lot of women and children; became B.C.'s first woman judge in 1917

H.R. MacMillan (1885-1976), forester, lumber executive; began a small timber export business in 1919, which expanded into a world leader and merged with another company to form MacMillan Bloedel, the largest lumber producer in Canada

Maquinna (?-c.1795), Nootka chief; was the main chief at Nootka Sound when Captain James Cook and other European explorers started visiting the area; an important middleman in the maritime fur trade, he managed to keep his people on friendly terms with both the Spanish and the British

Mungo Martin (1879-1962), born in Fort Rupert; Kwakiutl painter, carver, singer, songwriter; did much to rekindle pride in Native achievements and to preserve his people's culture by recording ancient songs; carved many totem poles

Margaret ("Ma") Murray (1888-1982), well-known, witty, outspoken publisher of *Bridge River-Lillooet News*; received Order of Canada, 1971

Wayne Ngan (1937-), born in China, lives on Hornby Island; artist; award-winning potter; a master of raku firing and salt glazes; uses elements of Chinese, Japanese and Korean ceramics

David See-Chai Lam

Dorothy Livesay

Sir Richard McBride

H.R. MacMillan

Maquinna

"Ma" Murray

Michael Smith

David Suzuki

Patricia Kathleen (P.K.) Page (1916-), born in England; writer, artist; moved to Victoria in 1964; won Governor General's Award for her poetry book *The Metal and the Flower*; her paintings and drawings are widely exhibited

Thomas Dufferin ("Duff") Pattullo (1873-1956), Ontario-born politician; came west in 1897; as Liberal premier (1933-41), started a vast program of public works, including a bridge across the Fraser at New Westminster, to create jobs during the Depression

Francis Rattenbury (1867-1935), born in England; architect; designed the legislative building, the Empress Hotel, and many other B.C. public buildings

William (Bill) Reid (1920-), born in Victoria; artist, sculptor, goldsmith; uses traditional Haida art forms, legends and designs in his own unique style; famous for works such as *The Spirit of Haida Gwaii*, a huge bronze canoe sculpture at the Canadian Embassy in Washington, D.C.; national speaker for Native rights

Alfred Scow (1927-), born in Alert Bay; judge; first Native person to become a lawyer in British Columbia; appointed provincial court judge in 1971; now a B.C. Roving Judge

Jack Shadbolt (1909-), raised in Victoria; artist, writer, teacher; one of Canada's most famous painters; uses primitive and modern styles; has written poetry and books about art

Gordon Shrum (1896-1985), physicist, professor; discovered the "green line" in the northern lights; professor and administrator at UBC for 36 years; first chancellor of Simon Fraser University; helped mastermind the Peace and Columbia rivers hydroelectric power projects

Michael Smith (1932-), born in England; professor, biochemist; came to UBC in 1966; developed ways to alter genes that are being used to fight cancer, create new plants, develop better medicines and build proteins to use in pulp and paper; co-winner of 1993 Nobel Prize for Chemistry

David Suzuki (1936-), born in Vancouver; scientist, educator, environmentalist, writer, broadcaster; widely known as host of CBC's science series *The Nature of Things*; author of many books, including his autobiography, *Metamorphosis: Stages in a Life*

Roy Henry Vickers (1946-), raised in a Nishga village; artist whose work reflects his mixed Tsimshian/Heiltsuk/British heritage; silk screens and wood sculptures known internationally

Ethel Wilson (1888-1980), born in South Africa; writer; moved to

Vancouver at age 10; her love of her adopted homeland showed in all her work; internationally acclaimed for several novels, in particular *Swamp Angel*

George Woodcock (1912-); literary journalist, historian, critic, writer; has written more than 60 books and edited 30 others on subjects ranging from history to literary criticism; included in his works are *British Columbia: A History of the Province* and two volumes of autobiography: *Letter to the Past* and *Beyond the Blue Mountains*

Ethel Wilson

Premiers of British Columbia

John Foster McCreight		1871-1872
Amor de Cosmos		1872-1874
George Anthony Walkem		1874-1876
Andrew Charles Elliott		1876-1878
George Anthony Walkem		1878-1882
Robert Beaven		1882-1883
William Smithe		1883-1887
Alexander. E.B. Davie	Conservative	1887-1889
John Robson	Liberal	1889-1892
Theodore Davie		1892-1895
John Herbert Turner		1895-1898
Charles August Semlin	Conservative	1898-1900
Joseph Martin	Liberal	1900
James Dunsmuir		1900-1902
Edward Gawler Prior	Conservative	1902-1903
Richard McBride	Conservative	1903-1915
William J. Bowser	Conservative	1915-1916
Harlan C. Brewster	Liberal	1916-1918
John Oliver	Liberal	1918-1927
John D. MacLean	Liberal	1927-1928
Simon F. Tolmie	Conservative	1928-1933
Thomas Dufferin Pattullo	Liberal	1933-1941
John Hart	Liberal (Coalition Government)	1941-1947
Byron I. Johnson	Liberal (Coalition Government)	1947-1952
W. A. C. Bennett	Social Credit	1952-1972
David Barrett	New Democratic Party	1972-1975
William R. Bennett	Social Credit	1975-1986
Wilhelmus "Bill" Vander Zalm	Social Credit	1986-1991
Rita Johnston	Social Credit	1991
Michael Harcourt	New Democratic Party	1991-

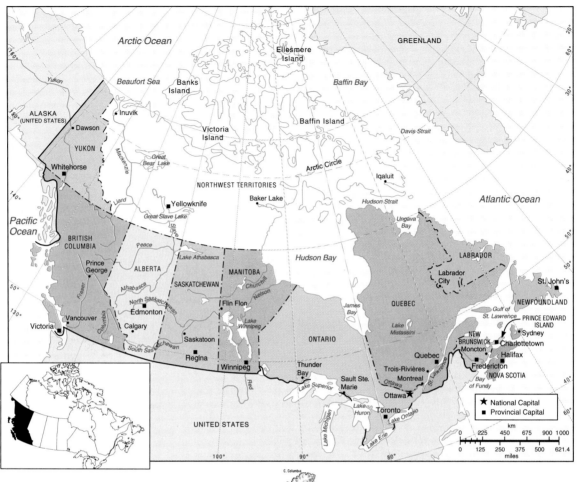

Arctic Ocean

GREENLAND

Ellesmere Island

Beaufort Sea

Banks Island

Baffin Bay

ALASKA (UNITED STATES)

Inuvik

Dawson

Victoria Island

Baffin Island

Davis Strait

Yukon

YUKON

Great Bear Lake

Arctic Circle

Iqaluit

Whitehorse

Mackenzie

NORTHWEST TERRITORIES

Atlantic Ocean

Liard

Hudson Strait

Ungava Bay

Pacific Ocean

Yellowknife

Baker Lake

Great Slave Lake

BRITISH COLUMBIA

Peace

Lake Athabasca

Hudson Bay

LABRADOR

Labrador City

Prince George

ALBERTA

Athabasca

SASKATCHEWAN

MANITOBA

Churchill

Nelson

St. John's

NEWFOUNDLAND

North Saskatchewan

Edmonton

Flin Flon

James Bay

QUEBEC

Gulf of St. Lawrence

PRINCE EDWARD ISLAND

Fraser

Columbia

Calgary

Lake Winnipeg

Lake Mistassini

Vancouver

Saskatoon

ONTARIO

Sydney

NEW BRUNSWICK

Charlottetown

Victoria

South Saskatchewan

Regina

Winnipeg

Quebec

Moncton

Halifax

Red

Thunder Bay

Trois-Rivières

Fredericton

Montreal

NOVA SCOTIA

Lake Superior

Sault Ste. Marie

Ottawa

St. Lawrence

Bay of Fundy

★ National Capital

UNITED STATES

Lake Michigan

Lake Huron

Toronto

Lake Ontario

Lake Erie

■ Provincial Capital

km
0   225   450   675   900 1000

miles
0   125   250   375   500 621.4

100°   90°   80°

Topography

QUEEN ELIZABETH ISLANDS

C. Columbia

Ellesmere Island

Pr. Patrick

Ellef Ringnes

Axel Heiberg

Bathurst

Melville

Beaufort Sea

Banks I.

Parry Channel

Devon I.

Somerset

Pr. of Wales

Bylot I.

Baffin Bay

Amundsen Gulf

Victoria Island

Boothia Pen.

G. of Boothia

Baffin Island

Great Bear Lake

Melville Pen.

Foxe Basin

Cumberland Sd.

Mt. Logan 19,524 ft. (5951 m.)

Mt. Fairweather 15,300 ft. (4663 m.)

Back

Wager Bay

Southampton I.

Hudson Str.

C. Chidley

Great Slave Lake

Coats I.

Mansel I.

Ungava Peninsula

Ungava Bay

QUEEN CHARLOTTE IS.

Peace

Athabasca

Reindeer L.

Churchill

Hudson Bay

Smallwood Res.

Churchill

Melville

Str. of Belle Isle

Queen Charlotte Sd.

Saskatchewan

Nelson

BELCHER IS.

Aki-miski

La Grande

Eastmain

Newfoundland

Avalon Pen.

Vancouver I.

Saskatchewan

PLATEAU

Île d'Anticosti

C. Race

Vancouver

Winnipegosis

Winnipeg

L. Manitoba

Nipissing

Mistassini

Gulf of St. Lawrence

Pr. Edward I.

Cape Breton I.

Regina

L. of the Woods

Lake Superior

Québec

Nova Scotia

Sable I.

Winnipeg

L. Nipigon

Montréal

Halifax

© Hammond Inc., Maplewood, N.J.

Ottawa

Manitoulin I.

Georgian Bay

Toronto

L. Huron

L. Ontario

Niagara Falls

5,000 m. 16,404 ft. | 2,000 m. 6,562 ft. | 1,000 m. 3,281 ft. | 500 m. 1,640 ft. | 200 m. 656 ft. | 100 m. 328 ft. | Sea Level | Below

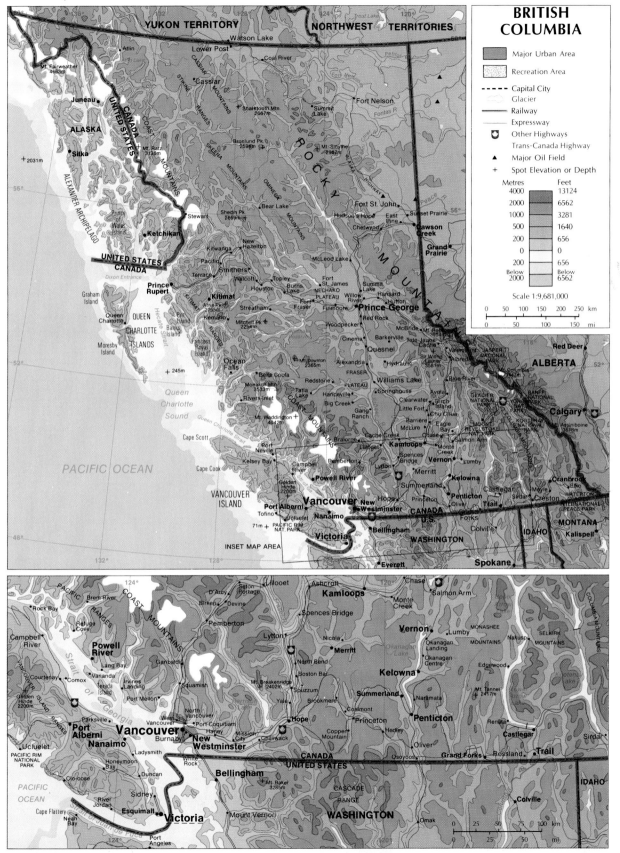

BRITISH COLUMBIA

Major Urban Area
Recreation Area
Capital City
Glacier
Railway
Expressway
Other Highways
Trans-Canada Highway
Major Oil Field
Spot Elevation or Depth

Metres	Feet
4000	13124
2000	6562
1000	3281
500	1640
200	656
0	0
200	656
Below 2000	Below 6562

Scale 1:9,681,000

0   50   100   150   200   250 km
0   50   100   150 mi

ECONOMY AND AGRICULTURE

ECONOMY

HEAVY INDUSTRY

- Aı Aluminum
- L Lead
- Z Zinc
- S Silver
- Transportation Equipment

LIGHT INDUSTRY

- Chemicals
- Food Processing
- Leather Products
- Lumber & Forest Products
- Pulp & Paper Products
- Water Power

OTHERS

- Fishing
- Seaport

MINING

- An Antimony
- C Coal
- Cu Copper
- G Gold
- I Iron Ore
- L Lead
- Gs Natural Gas
- Pm Petroleum
- S Silver
- Sn Tin
- Tu Tungsten
- Z Zinc

AGRICULTURE

- Feed Grains & Livestock
- Fruit & General Farming (Irrigated)
- Fruit, Truck & General Farming
- Dairy Farming
- Grazing & Other Livestock
- Forests

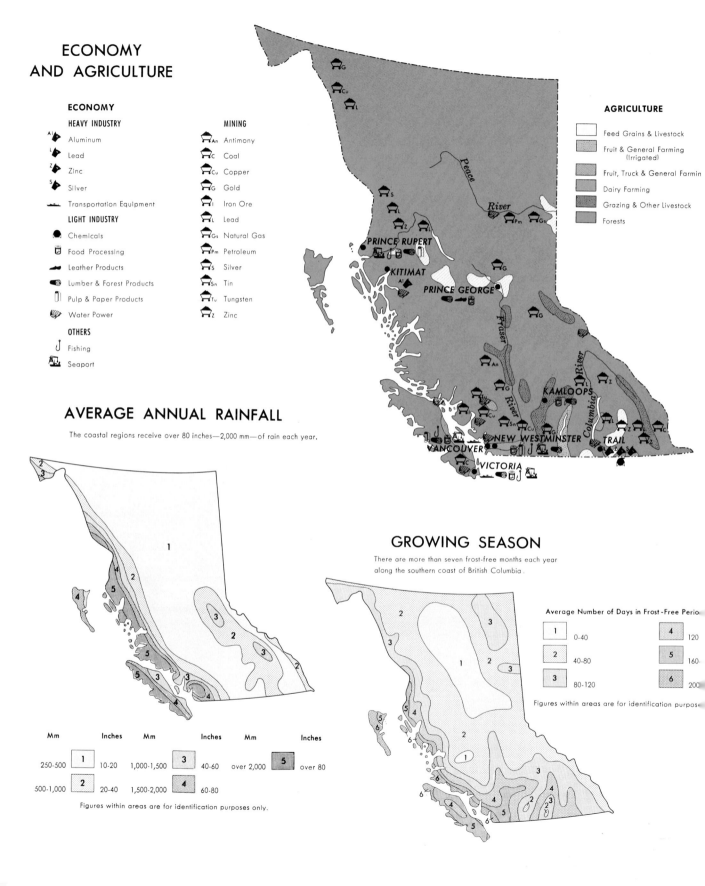

PRINCE RUPERT
KITIMAT
PRINCE GEORGE
KAMLOOPS
NEW WESTMINSTER
TRAIL
VANCOUVER
VICTORIA

Peace River
Fraser River
Columbia River

AVERAGE ANNUAL RAINFALL

The coastal regions receive over 80 inches—2,000 mm—of rain each year.

Mm		Inches	Mm		Inches	Mm		Inches
250-500	1	10-20	1,000-1,500	3	40-60	over 2,000	5	over 80
500-1,000	2	20-40	1,500-2,000	4	60-80			

Figures within areas are for identification purposes only.

GROWING SEASON

There are more than seven frost-free months each year along the southern coast of British Columbia.

Average Number of Days in Frost-Free Period

1	0-40		4	120
2	40-80		5	160
3	80-120		6	200

Figures within areas are for identification purposes

Index

About the Author/Editors

Isabel Nanton is a writer and photographer living in Vancouver. She has written *Adventuring in British Columbia,* now in its fourth printing, and also teaches travel writing at UBC's Continuing Education Dept.

Nancy Flight, West Coast Editorial Associates (WCEA), has worked in book publishing since 1972, editing both trade books and textbooks at all levels.

Barbara Tomlin, WCEA, has been a freelance editor since 1978. She also has taught university English and workshops in editing and proofreading.

Yvonne Van Ruskenveld, WCEA, has been a freelance editor and writer for business, government, non-profit and academic clients since 1987.

Lois Richardson, WCEA, has worked in publishing since 1975 as a journalist and magazine editor. She is the author of two non-fiction books.

Picture acknowledgments

Abbreviations for location on page are, alone or in combination: T = Top, M = Middle, B = Bottom, L = Left, R = Right, I = Inset, BG Background.

Front cover, 8-9, 11 (all), 13L, 16T/BR, 17BL/BR, 21IL, 22ML, 35TL, 81I, 84R, 87 (both), 118TL, 121 (bird), **Graham Osborne;** 2-3, 21BG, 81BG, 111TL/R, 121L, 127, Derek Trask/**The Stock Market Inc., Toronto;** 4, 16BL, 35TR, 62, 70, 72, 78, 80L, 83 (all), 84L, 85R, 89R, 90R, 100L, 106TL/BL, 108BR, 110R, 115L, 120 (both), 131, George Hunter/**Ivy Photo;** 5, 14R, 22TR/TL/BR/BL, 33TL/TM, 113IL/IR, 115TR, 122 (flower), Menno Fieguth/**Ivy Photo:** 6, 21IR, 22MR, 35BR, 61L, 71, 76R, 89L, 92B, 100L, 103 (both), 106TR/MR, 108T, 110L, 113BG, 116T, 118BG, Malak/**Ivy Photo;** 13R, 14L, 25R, 33TR, 35BL, 68, 75L, 76TL, 80R, 90L, 92MR, 111BL, 115BR, 116B, 117R, 118TR, 121R, 125, 129, back cover, **Ivy Photo;** 17T, **Tourism B.C.;** 19L, **Charles Russell;** 19TR, Norman Lightfoot/**Ivy Photo;** 19BR, Leonard Lee Rue III/**Ivy Photo;** 25L, **Royal Ontario Museum;** 27 (both), **Gerald Lazare and Lewis Parker;** 29 (53094 C6124), 30L (HP54020), 40L, 45 (both), 46, 48, 49, 132MT (70606), 133MT (20328 D6009), 136T (7931), 134T, 135MB/MT, **British Columbia Archives;** 30R, 54TL, 108BL, Peter d'Angelo/**Ivy Photo;** 33BL, **National Museums of Canada;** 36, 39, 43, 47, **The Confederation Life Gallery of Canadian History;** 40R, **Native Sons of British Columbia;** 50 (C11040), 52T (C3693), 52B (C16715), 54TR, (PA17193), 56L (C12035), 132T (C36048), 133MB (PA25397), **National Archives of Canada;** 54B, 59, 61R, **Vancouver City Archives;** 56R (6232), 64 (1276), 67R (26804), **Vancouver Public Library;** 67L, © **Claude Detloff;** 76BL, **Jeff Vinnick;** 85L, Dave Butler/**Skyline Images;** 92T, Andrew Catlin/**Courtesy A & M Records;** 92ML, 99R, **Art Gallery of Ontario;** 95L, **Courtesy the Bard on the Beach Society;** 95R, **Courtesy CBC-TV;** 96B, **Tourism Victoria;** 96T, **Rocky Mountains Visitors' Association;** 97L, David Cooper/**Courtesy The Vancouver Opera;** 97R, Andrew Waddy/**Courtesy Kokoro Dance;** 99R, Courtesy Jack Shadbolt; 104L, Courtesy The B.C. Lions; 104R, Courtesy The **Vancouver Canucks;** 105L, **Canapress;** 105M/R, Bill Cunningham/**B.C. Sports Hall of Fame;** 106BR, Paul Gilbert/**The Stock Market Inc., Toronto;** 117L, 118I, W. Lowry/**Visual Contact;** 122BG, Wilf Schurig/**Ivy Photo;** 132MB, **University of Western Ontario;** 132B, 135MB, 137, **University of British Columbia;** 133T, **Progressive Conservative Party;** 133B, **Columbia Artists Management Inc.;** 134MT, **National Health and Welfare Information Services;** 134MB, **Canadian Sports Images;** 135T, **Office of the Lieutenant-Governor;** 135MT, **Department of Archives and Special Collections, University of Manitoba;** 135B, **MacMillan Bloedel;** 136B, Fred Phipps Photo/**Courtesy CBC-TV.**